SEASONS OF A DEAN'S LIFE

SEASONS OF A
DEAN'S LIFE

Understanding the Role and
Building Leadership Capacity

*Walt Gmelch, Dee Hopkins,
and Sandra Damico*

1996–2011 15TH ANNIVERSARY

Sty/us
PUBLISHING, LLC.

STERLING, VIRGINIA

COPYRIGHT © 2011 BY
STYLUS PUBLISHING, LLC.

Published by Stylus Publishing, LLC
22883 Quicksilver Drive
Sterling, Virginia 20166-2102

Library of Congress Cataloging-in-Publication Data
Gmelch, Walter H.
Seasons of a dean's life : understanding the role and building
leadership capacity / Walt Gmelch, Dee Hopkins, and
Sandra Damico.
    p. cm.
    Includes bibliographical references and index.
    ISBN 978-1-57922-318-2 (cloth : alk. paper)
    ISBN 978-1-57922-319-9 (pbk. : alk. paper)
    ISBN 978-1-57922-728-9 (library networkable e-edition :
alk. paper)
    ISBN 978-1-57922-729-6 (consumer e-edition : alk. paper)
    1. Deans (Education)   2. Universities and
colleges—Administration.   3. Educational leadership.
I. Hopkins, Dee.   II. Damico, Sandra.   III. Title.
LB2341.G564   2011
378.1'11—dc23   2011017097

13-digit ISBN: 978-1-57922-318-2 (cloth)
13-digit ISBN: 978-1-57922-319-9 (paper)
13-digit ISBN: 978-1-57922-728-9 (library networkable
e-edition)
13-digit ISBN: 978-1-57922-729-6 (consumer e-edition)

Printed in the United States of America

All first editions printed on acid free paper
that meets the American National Standards Institute
Z39-48 Standard.

Bulk Purchases

Quantity discounts are available for
use in workshops and for staff
development.
Call 1-800-232-0223

First Edition, 2011

10   9   8   7   6   5   4   3   2   1

A good while ago, there were four of us who became deans: Walt and Sandy in Iowa, Dee in South Dakota, and Judy in Washington. We also became friends. Through the years, Dee moved on to deanships in Texas, then to West Virginia, and Walt moved to California. As we became accustomed to being deans and our knowledge of the role grew, we began sharing our experiences and expertise with others. Walt presented chair and dean workshops all over the country for the American Council on Education (ACE) and the American Association of Colleges for Teacher Education (AACTE). Judy joined him as a presenter for AACTE for several years. Sandy and Dee were active in the Women in the Deanship Special Study Group of AACTE and presented leadership development sessions every summer for sitting deans and those aspiring to become deans. The four of us led sessions, year after year, at professional conferences, including AACTE and the American Educational Research Association (AERA) always on leadership, specifically the many aspects of deans as leaders.

And, from the beginning, after every leadership presentation, we continually reminded one another, "We ought to write a book." For years, we collected data, interviewed our colleagues, and wrote proposals and gave presentations on leadership, specifically as it applied to deans.

Finally, as Sandy and Judy began talking retirement, we decided to buckle down and get the book written. When we met at conferences, we saved time to discuss "the book." And we made progress but not a lot; as sitting deans we were busy people. Other priorities took precedence.

Then, on June 26, 2009, our friend and colleague, Dr. Judy Mitchell, died unexpectedly, and the three of us decided that, regardless of our busy schedules, this book needed to be finished. It became the priority. Originally, each of us had responsibility for one season of the deanship. Sandy was responsible for the springtime; Dee, summer; Walt, fall; and Judy, winter. With Judy's untimely passing, it has been necessary for us to write her season, so we utilized her notes from the many workshops and leadership sessions she had prepared through the years to assist us.

Remembering the countless individuals Judy mentored through the years, the number she groomed for leadership roles, and the important place she held in the hearts of so many, we felt it only fitting to dedicate this book to Dr. Judy Mitchell, a true leader, inspiring professional, and most especially, our dear friend.

Walt Gmelch, Dee Hopkins, Sandy Damico
February 14, 2011

CONTENTS

I

THE DEVELOPMENT OF
DEANS AS LEADERS

Introduction

The development of academic leaders is at a critical juncture. While the corporate world complains that they simply have progressed from the Bronze Age of leadership to the Iron Age, we fear higher education may still be in the Dark Ages. The purpose of this book is, hopefully, to help illuminate the way to the Building Age of academic leadership capacity. To accomplish this, we look to those who are serving, or have served, in leadership roles—specifically deans—to see if their personal experiences and development could shed light on how the leadership skills of future deans might be cultivated. Our investigation included (a) interviewing over 50 sitting deans, (b) conducting professional development seminars for several hundred deans, and (c) reflecting on our personal 50 years of collective experience in 10 different deanships. By tracing our own and others' administrative journeys, we found similarities in how deans progressed as leaders—especially over time. We also found definite stages or "seasons" of the deanship from (a) getting started—the first three years of deanship (springtime), (b) hitting your stride—years four to seven of deanship (summer), (c) keeping the fire alive—eight years and beyond of deanship (fall), to (d) ending of an era—life after deaning (winter). Though we found it possible to track the progression of deans throughout the seasons, we were unable to identify any continuum of specific, formalized leadership development that all deans were expected to experience along the way. The mastery of these academic executives appears to be left to chance. Although this may be just benign neglect, higher education institutions need to realize this lack may negatively impact a dean's success.

This book is designed to provide the reader with deeper understanding of the leadership development needed, and obtained, by deans as they progress through their academic careers. Chapter 1 discusses the need for skillful deans, the transitions they encounter as they progress toward mastery, the rites of passage they must undergo along the way, and the seasons of their academic life. Chapters 2 through 5 each discuss a season, providing an in-depth picture of a specific time span of a dean's academic life. Examples, shared by sitting and previous deans in which they discuss their personal leadership successes and failures, give the reader a taste of what the deanship is really like—and how it changes as one spends more time in the role. Numerous anecdotal reflections are included in these chapters as well. Chapter 6 pulls it all together and reflects on the deanship continuum, the seasons of a dean's academic life.

The Deanship: Passages in the Profession

Scholars and administrators alike speak about a great leadership crisis in higher education. Blue ribbon commissions and executive reports, including the American Council on Education (Eckel, Hill, & Green, 1998), the Kellogg Commission (1999), the Kellogg Foundation (1999), and the Global Consortium of Higher Education (Acker, 1999), to name a few, call for bolder and better college and university leadership. The search for solutions to this leadership dilemma leads us to realize that the dean as academic leader is one of the least studied and most misunderstood management positions in America. The transformation to true mastery of academic leadership takes time, training, and commitment, and not all deans make the complete transition.

Stages of Leadership Development

Before we can define how deans become master leaders, it is necessary to ascertain the social and psychological stages they experience as they progress through the seasons of their deanships. The majority begin their journey as faculty. Some choose to go into administration; others find themselves in an administrative role unexpectedly—sometimes merely because they are in the right place at the right time. Regardless of the route, new deans must grow and develop if their skill as leaders is to continually improve.

There is an extensive body of research on the stages of development of children and adolescents, but what about adult development? Until a couple of decades ago, developmental charting stopped around age 21—as if adults escape any further distinguishable stages of development. Three prominent life-cycle scholars, Roger Gould of the University of California–Los Angeles (UCLA), Yale psychologist Daniel Levinson, and George Vaillant of Harvard, have developed theories about adult development. These theories, popularly written in Gail Sheehy's books *Passages* (1976) and *New Passages* (1995), and professionally reported in Daniel Levinson's *The Seasons of a Man's Life* (1978) and Roger Gould's *Transformations* (1978), outline remarkably predictable crises of adulthood. Transition to and from each of these stages in adult life brings about change, whether it is the exhilaration of a new appointment in the academy or depression from the denial of tenure. The literature on the development of adults is inconsistent, and none of it is particularly useful in describing the professional development of deans. Although we don't propose to present a developmental theory of the deanship, we did discover a number of similarities experienced by deans as they moved through the four seasons.

Passages of the Profession

Gail Sheehy observes in her book *New Passages* that in the span of the last generation, the life cycle has been significantly altered. People leave childhood sooner, take longer to grow up, and much longer to grow old. During most of human history, only 1 in 10 individuals lived to the age of 65. Today, the average American is 38 and will live to 78, although there are differences by race and ethnicity (Gergen, 1990; Hodgkinson, 2002).

Now, in contemporary America, 8 in 10 individuals sail past their 65th birthdays and do not even slow down. For many, this ensures time on the job to be markedly increased before retirement. It also allows individuals to experience not just one or two careers in their adult life, but four or five. So how does this impact the professoriate, or more specifically, the deanship? Are chief executive officers of schools and colleges remaining longer in the job, or are they choosing to leave the profession, taking their administrative skills to industry, politics, or community service? Are they going back into the classroom after fulfilling leadership roles or do they jump at retirement as soon as possible?

These questions cannot be taken lightly. Their impact is felt daily in institutions of higher learning. Whether the choice is retirement, teaching, or a new career outside academe, the pool of experienced leaders competent to enter the deanship is dwindling. Numerous commissions and executive reports point to the dearth of leadership throughout higher education. Several years ago, Dale Andersen, a former American Association of Colleges for Teacher Education (AACTE) president, oversaw the AACTE Leadership Recruitment Services. Created by AACTE to serve as a referral and connection to assist institutions seeking candidates and individuals interested in leadership positions, it is no longer in existence; however, while Andersen was working with them, he noted the difficulty institutions have in filling deans' positions—often going through three or four cycles before finding viable candidates. Andersen further noted the repercussions of those unfilled positions: institutions suffering from lack of leadership, colleges suffering from lack of representation, faculty suffering from lack of a strong voice of advocacy, states suffering from lack of connection and communication, and the profession suffering from the void that is temporally created (Andersen, 2002).

Andersen's observations continue to be relevant. We interviewed a number of search firm consultants, asking them about the breadth and depth of today's applicant pools. We also asked them if they were seeing any change in the participation rate and makeup of applicant pools and, if so, why. Finally, we asked them to share their observations about the evolution of the deanship, if they thought the position held the appeal it might have in the past, and whether it was becoming more difficult for them to do their job and match suitable candidates to institutions seeking leadership.

Synthesizing their responses, we found that most agreed the pools of applicants have shrunk over the last decade. One headhunter attributed the decline to candidate selectivity, pointing out social, economic, financial, and personal reasons. Another remarked that the normal pipeline of individuals who fill deanships (i.e., chairs, directors, and assistant and associate deans) is not deep.

The consultants shared with us the concerns they hear from likely candidates, commenting that many more than in the past are reluctant to move from established positions. Reasons given include the economy in general and, more specifically, budget cuts in higher education nationwide. A number of possible candidates are convinced that staying put is the best option regardless of their desire to climb the academic ladder. "Lately, when I try to recruit, the number one reason I hear from many qualified applicants as to why they won't apply is their fear that they won't be able to sell their house or, even if they do, having to take a substantial loss." Additionally, with banks less eager to lend, financing new houses poses problems for prospective candidates.

Other reluctant individuals cite family obligations such as needing to stay near aging parents or their children's school. Some are fearful that spousal support or partner accommodation won't be guaranteed at another institution. Still others worry about moving costs, insurance benefits, and retirement matches. Overall, today's "would-be" candidates are paying a lot closer attention to the financial well-being of their own institutions as well as the stability of any they might consider serving.

Search professionals also point to professional considerations in accounting for the shrinking size of candidate pools. Academic leadership positions themselves seem to hold less appeal for the tenured professors whom institutions would recruit to fill them. Potential candidates point out that the actual duties—particularly attracting external support and broadly overseeing personnel—amount to a substantial increase in working hours without a commensurate increase in compensation.

Couple this candidate reluctance with the graying of existing administration and we may see future candidate pools become even more shallow. Consultants noted that 30% of the current presidents and provosts (baby boomers) will be eligible to retire in the next three to five years. This trickle-down effect is already noticeable in higher education as institutions attempt to find quality applicants for upper administrative posts. Community colleges in many states are already struggling to attract deans.

One search consultant commented on the influx of international applicants in the searches he is conducting. He shared that half of the attendees at a recent "so you want to be a dean" workshop that his firm held were internationals from India and Asia. Although language is a major barrier for a number of these individuals, a future trend may find our nation's institutions looking to an international pipeline for their future leadership.

Have the responsibilities of the deanship become so insurmountable that many are opting out early—or never entering at all? The current climate of reform has changed the role of all education leaders. Functioning in a rapidly changing world, they are expected to show marked and continual improvement quickly and with fewer resources (King, 2002). As deans, they are no longer staid academicians. Rather, the positions have expanded beyond ivy-covered walls to resemble contemporary chief executive officers of industry.

Their current responsibilities demand skills that were not associated or emphasized with the deanship previously. One example, possibly exacerbated by the economy, is the expectation that deans will produce substantial financial gains for their colleges and institutions through their fundraising, grant, and earmark obtainment. In spite of the broadening of the deanship position, preparation for it appears to be no further along than it was a generation ago. In 1980, Corbally and Holmberg-Wright pointed out that no ideal pattern or model for academic administration had emerged. Most deans learned their skills on a "catch-as-catch-can" basis along with a "sink-or-swim" approach to administrative assignments. For many, that is still the norm and, in reality, most deans continue to be self-taught professionals (Gmelch, 2000).

Colleges are almost impossible to manage, and academics who are trying to run or repair them are getting "burned out and eased out with astonishing speed" (O'Reilly, 1994, p. 64). Is that true? What is happening to deans? Are they taking on the role sooner than before with less experience than in the past? How long do deans stay? Has the position become so demanding that many retire earlier, change careers, or go back into the classroom? Are deans burning out more quickly than their predecessors? What is the professional life span of today's dean? And, more importantly, can the reasons for its length, or brevity, be pinpointed?

Trends in the Dean Position and Requirements

Changes in the deanship stem from alterations in the academic institutions themselves, insofar as they control and posit the position duties and requirements of their deans and dean candidates, and the nature of the candidates for those positions, both individually and collectively.

From an institutional perspective, the requirements and duties of deans have undergone significant changes in recent years. A random sample of 50 advertisements in *The Chronicle of Higher Education* from September to December in both 2004 and 2009 reveals profound differences in both the requirements of eligible candidates and the postulated duties of eventual deans. Contrary to the anecdotal evidence provided by the deans we interviewed reflecting fundraising skills growing in importance, the advertisement samples show that the profile of demonstrated fundraising ability fell significantly from 2004 to 2009 as a requirement for deanship candidates. Trending upward, meanwhile, in requisite qualifications for dean candidates were the profiles of both intangible qualities like "vision" and indices of professional accomplishment, such as having achieved "tenure status."

Relying upon the advertised needs, it appears the duties of deanships did shift significantly between 2004 and 2009. In 2004, the two most commonly cited tasks that deans could expect to undertake were "fundraising" and "leadership." In 2009, "fundraising" and "leadership" continued to feature prominently in job descriptions but were trumped by "vision" and "program development." Again, flying in the face of the anecdotal evidence available, the status of fundraising as both an explicit requirement of candidates and duty of eventual deans fell markedly between 2004 and 2009. Replacing it in prominence as both a requirement and a duty was the much more nebulous "vision" of the candidate and eventual dean. The sample of 2009 job postings depicts the ideal candidate for a deanship as already possessing firm beliefs about what a given institution should do or should be, rather than merely implementing policy from above and attracting external support. In fact, although the 2009 requirements for candidates were as rigorous and specific as those in 2004, the 2009 job descriptions were vastly less specific than those in 2004. Colleges and universities appeared much less willing to provide explicit direction to incoming academic leaders. Rather than providing guidance to new deans, then, the institutions seem themselves to expect such guidance from the very candidates that they would hire.

Institutions of higher education require an increasingly strong leader, task that leader with an ever-broadening range of responsibilities, and are perpetually less explicit in terms of their concrete expectations of that leader. Both in professional and in economic terms, then, the opportunity cost of assuming a deanship has risen significantly in recent years. Such a picture implies that the rapid burnout experienced by many might well result not from significant changes in the candidates hired into deanships, but rather from the shifting nature of the dean positions themselves. With increasingly arduous and yet vague duties facing incoming deans, the topic of dean development, with a particular eye toward achieving mastery while avoiding burnout, becomes of great importance to the field.

The Development of Academic Deans

Although Garbarro says it takes up to two and a half years to master the executive position (Garbarro, 1985), and Gmelch posits that an outside dean will need a year and a half to begin to become competent in a new deanship (Gmelch, 2000), executive development is difficult to determine. One of the most glaring shortcomings in the leadership development area is the scarcity of sound research on how and when to train and develop leaders (Conger & Benjamin, 1999). Gmelch (2002) contends that leadership development is a process that extends over many years. Rather than search for answers in specific training programs, he suggests that three spheres of influence create the conditions essential to develop masterful academic deans: (a) conceptual understanding of the unique roles and responsibilities encompassed in the deanship; (b) the skills necessary to achieve the results through working with faculty, staff, students, constituents, and campus leaders; and (c) reflective practice to learn from past experiences and perfect the art of leadership. Using these three spheres and their intersections (Figure 1.1) as our analytical framework, let's discuss how strong academic deans might be developed (adapted from Gmelch & Miskin, 2011; Wolverton & Gmelch, 2002).

FIGURE 1.1
Dean Leadership Development

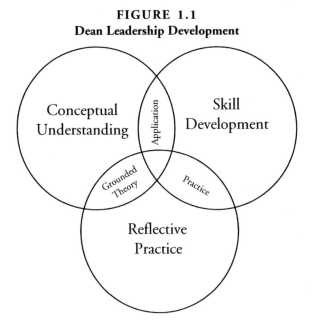

Conceptual Understanding

Conceptual knowledge or understanding is the ability to envision the leadership role of the dean. Cognitively, deans can develop their skills as leaders if they explore and understand their role by using mental models, frameworks, and role theory to reveal the many dimensions of leadership (Conger & Benjamin, 1999). Two issues are most important here: (a) as deans move into leadership positions, their conceptualization of the job of dean shifts, and (b) although some commonalities exist across all types of organizations, many of the challenges deans in institutions of higher education face are not typical of chief executive officers in business and leaders in other organizations.

First, as academics move into the deanship from previous positions in the academy, they start to perceive themselves differently. For example, using Bolman and Deal's terms (2008), department chairpersons, the pool from which most deans are drawn, predominantly think in terms of the human and structural frames of leadership (Gmelch, Reason, Schuh, & Shelley, 2002). Their focus is on people, keeping the staff happy, helping faculty progress toward tenure, assisting groups as they revise curriculum. They are also attentive to structure. As the keepers of the rules, they make sure their people are aware of policies and adhere to them.

As they move into the deanship, however, two new frames, the political and the symbolic, demand greater attention. Suddenly the ceremonies, graduations, and honors dinners they conveniently skipped when they were faculty or chairs become high priorities. Compromise becomes more important and they begin to see the importance of interrelationships and become big-picture people.

Second, the dimensions of leadership may be different, given the context and organizational conditions of the colleges and universities. Although deans' roles may resemble those of other executives (Helgesen, 1990; Mintzberg, 1973), some are also particular to the university (Jackson, 2002). Unlike many executives, deans serve external and political constituencies, manage college resources, promote internal productivity, and attend to personnel matters, all while engaging in personal scholarship and keeping a semblance of their faculty role alive.

Skill Development

Although having a conceptual understanding of the deanship is a necessary condition a dean must have in order to lead, it is insufficient without the application of appropriate behaviors and skills. So, what are the skills that are most critical for deans to succeed? Planning and prioritizing? Visioning? Resolving conflict? Managing resources? Motivating faculty and staff? Team building? We contend that all of these are critical and that they raise and lower in level of importance depending upon the current demands of the college. For example, if the college has suffered cutbacks—financial or human resources—managing resources and motivating faculty and staff become priorities. If the college is flush and everyone seems content, it may be a great time for visioning, planning, and prioritizing. Equal in their importance, all of the skills are essential; a masterful dean, ever watchful of the college climate, juggles the skills most needed when the time is right.

So, how do deans develop these essential skills for success? They can attend formal learning opportunities, including seminars, workshops, and lectures, and utilize simulations, case studies, and action planning to hone their skills. Many training opportunities for deans are designed to have institutions send their midmanagers off-site for a three- or four-day retreat. These are effective in instilling key ingredients for skill development; however, research has shown that this type of skill development is more effective when work teams and their associates attend the programs together (Conger, 1992). This is not always feasible, nor is it always appropriate, especially for a new dean who is trying to establish himself or herself. As previously noted, when an individual becomes dean, his or her role changes. So do his or her relationships—especially if he or she was promoted internally and enjoyed faculty colleagues as friends. Within each institutional culture, a new dean must first be seen as "the dean" before a strong leadership team can be established. Then and only then will development of the "team" be most beneficial.

Formal training is only one part of acquiring skills to be a dean. Deans also require on-the-job practical experience before they are able to translate their knowledge into skills. According to an ancient Buddhist philosopher, to know and not to use is not yet to know.

Reflective Practice

A dean's leadership development trek is an inner journey. Self-knowledge, personal awareness, and personal corrective feedback must be part of a dean's progression through the seasons of his or her career. Moral, ethical, and spiritual dimensions need to be included in the dean's travel pack. They are necessary components for any successful dean to complete the trek. Dean development is very much about finding one's voice (Kouzes & Posner, 1987, 2006; Matusak, 1997). Because credibility and authenticity lie at the heart of the deanship, the ability to determine one's own guiding beliefs and assumptions undergirds the effective dean. By listening to structured feedback, reflecting often, and developing self-awareness, conditions can be created for thoughtful deans to flourish.

Donald Schon, in his book *The Reflective Practitioner* (1983), contends that reflection-in-action is central to dealing well with uncertainty, instability, uniqueness, and value conflict—common occurrences in deans' leadership lives. For this reason alone, the use of reflection-in-action is critically important. Deans' isolation in their respective positions works against reflection. Although managers do reflect-in-action, deans seldom reflect on their own observations (Schon, 1983, p. 243). That is why deans need to establish strong support networks in which they feel safe to communicate their private dilemmas and insights and are able to test them against the views of their peers. Leadership development does not occur in a vacuum (Beineke & Sublett, 1999). Its nurturing flourishes best within a group or with trusted colleagues acting as mentors, partners, and coaches.

In sum, dean development must incorporate all three approaches: conceptual development, skill building, and reflective practice. Chapter 6 of this book highlights strategies that can foster dean leadership development across personal, institutional, and professional levels—and throughout the seasons of a dean's life.

Rites of Passage: The Seasons of a Dean's Career

Traditional tribal societies place tremendous emphasis on transitions in their social culture, as did ancient civilizations. Arnold van Gennep, a Dutch anthropologist, first interpreted these rites for a modern, Western audience almost 85 years ago. He coined the term "rites of passage" to describe the way rites were used in traditional societies to structure life transitions dealing with birth, puberty, death, selection of a chief, and creation of the shaman (Bridges, 1980; van Gennep, 1960). Although appointing a new dean is not equivalent to anointing a shaman, both transitions pass through three phases: separation, transition, and incorporation. The first phase consists of separating one from the old and familiar social context and putting the person through a symbolic death experience. For an individual accepting a first deanship, the awareness of this separation may come when he or she is no longer asked to join the group for pizza and beer after work—even though he or she had been an active participant in the past. Next comes a time in isolation in what van Gennep called the "neutral zone," a gap between the old way of being and the new. As the months go by, the new dean realizes his or her previous peer group has disappeared. Now recognized as the "boss," it is impossible for him or her to share a personal opinion—especially about faculty, staff, or students—with anyone within the college. Even going to lunch with a faculty member can be, and often is, construed as favoritism. Finally, when the intended inner changes have taken place, a person is brought back and reenters the social order on a new basis. "New" drops from the description and he or she becomes "the dean." The new dean sees the college through a different lens and focuses on the big picture rather than his or her previous content area or department. Different peers are found among fellow deans on campus or in similar roles in other institutions. All passage rites are revealed in this three-phase form. Rituals of passage are simply a way of focusing and making more visible the natural pattern of dying, chaos, and renewal. Recently, transition management writer William Bridges used van Gennep's cultural transition research to examine the three natural phases of job transitions: *endings,* the *neutral zone,* and the *new beginnings* (1980, 1991).

Sociologists label this transition period from the time of appointment to a position until the time of acceptance in the organization as the *organizational socialization* period. From the many organizational socialization developmental models (Hart, 1993), a similar three-stage model emerges: (a) *anticipation,* (b) *encounter,* and (c) *adaptation.* The anticipatory socialization stage begins when an individual is selected for the new position as dean and has made the decision to leave the current position as characterized by breaking off loyalties to the present position and developing new loyalties. Louis (1980) refers to this as *leave taking.* The encounter stage begins when one actually starts the new position and begins to cope with the routines, surprises, and relationships of a new college, new institution, and possibly a new state. Finally, the adaptation stage begins when one develops strong, trusting relationships in the new role and new location and finds out how things work in the new organization.

This theoretical framework has been used to study new department chairs as they transition from faculty to administration (Gmelch & Parkay,

1999; Gmelch & Seedorf, 1989; Seedorf, 1990), as well as the socialization process new school administrators go through (Ortiz, 1982), and is the basis for this current study on academic deans.

Book Objectives

The purpose of this book is to explore the rites of passage academic deans experience as they enter and transition through their deanships. Because most deans usually come to their positions without leadership training, without prior executive experience, without a clear understanding of the ambiguity of their new roles, without recognition of the metamorphic changes they will undergo, and without an awareness of the toll their new positions will take on their academic and personal lives, we hope to provide our readers with an overview of what they will experience as they grow and develop in their leadership role. Borrowing from Sheehy, we have traced the journey of many sitting and previous deans as they progressed through the seasons of their academic career. Specifically, we investigated several questions leading to how deans successfully made the transition to the deanship and beyond:

1. What socialization process do academics go through to get settled into a new deanship?
2. What are the keys for successful entry and rite of passage into the deanship?
3. What critical events shape how deans progress through the stages of the deanship?
4. What individual and organizational strategies and tactics do deans use in their periods of transition?
5. What surprises and challenges do deans face at different stages of their deanship?
6. What can new deans, universities, and faculties do to make the transition to, through, and out of the deanship more successful and productive?

The literature is too often silent on these questions of leadership succession, at least from the leader's perspective (Sorenson, 2000). It is our hope that this book with its focus on the development and socialization process of deans as they journey through the seasons of their academic careers will provide practical advice and strategies for success for the deans who will follow.

Research Design

This case study of deans was undertaken to investigate the organizational socialization process of deans and draw practical implications for institutions and academic leaders. Four researchers conducted in-depth interviews of 50 deans at different stages (seasons) of the deanship—similar to the anticipation, encounter, and adaptation phases: (a) getting started, (b) hitting your stride, (c) keeping the fire alive, and (d) life after deaning. In addition, they questioned well over 100 dean colleagues during workshops and professional conferences to ascertain their attitudes and understanding of the role. Finally, with over 50 years of collective time on the job at multiple institutions, they included their own life experiences. This methodological approach, grounded in the interpretive perspective (Morgan, 1980) advocated by MacPherson, rests on the premise that to understand the socialization process, it is necessary to "understand an administrator's sense of 'being an administrator' over time in terms of what he or she does and his or her reflections on what is being done" (MacPherson, 1984, p. 60). The few studies that have been conducted on the deanship have treated the position as though it was an undifferentiated experience across time. Our experience indicated that this was not so. But, if the position as dean holds different rewards and stresses depending upon length of time a person is in the deanship, what exactly are these differences? The interview procedure permitted the deans to report on their routine and nonroutine impressions of the deanship as well as their perspectives, beliefs, and overall sense making (Staton-Spicer & Spicer, 1987).

Sample and Procedures

An open-ended interview guide was developed based upon the literature and our experiences as well as those of some of our colleagues. In order to be able to compare responses across the sample, a core set of questions was developed for use with all those interviewed. For each season of a dean's life, we then developed a series of unique questions.

Of the 50 individuals formally interviewed, 33 were men and 17 were women. The sample included five African-Americans and seven Latinos. Not all of those interviewed were education deans; business, arts and sciences, and human science deans also participated in the study. Of particular interest is the range of professional fields from which education deans are drawn. Common lore would have one believe that deans primarily have educational administration backgrounds. In this study, less than half of the deans reported their professional field as educational administration. Of these deans, 20 were deans in their 9th to 13th years in the position. Those deans who have made the move to a deanship more recently report a wide range of professional disciplines; only two between their 1st and 8th year in the deanship came from an educational administration background.

A convenience sampling of education and human development deans were interviewed for this study; all those approached agreed to be interviewed. Across the sample, interviews ranged from 45 to 90 minutes, with most taking an hour. Interviews were conducted in person and over the phone. Two of the interviewers took notes and then transcribed them, one also audiotaped the interviews and had them transcribed, and one typed interview responses into a computer during the interview process.

References

Acker, D. (Ed.). (1999). *Leadership for higher education in agriculture.* Ames: Iowa State University, Global Consortium of Higher Education and Research for Agriculture.

Andersen, D. A. (2002). The deans of the future. In W. H. Gmelch (Ed.), *Deans balancing act: Education leaders and the challenges they face.* Washington, DC: AACTE Publications

Beineke, J. A., & Sublett, R. H. (1999). *Leadership lessons and competencies: Learning from the Kellogg National Fellowship Program.* Battle Creek, MI: Kellogg Foundation.

Bolman, L. G., & Deal, T. E. (2008). *Reframing organizations* (4th ed.). San Francisco: Jossey-Bass.

Bridges, W. (1980). *Transitions: Making sense of life's changes.* Reading, MA: Addison Wesley.

Bridges, W. (1991). *Managing transitions.* Reading, MA: Perseus Books.

Conger, J. A. (1992). *Learning to lead: The art of transforming managers into leaders.* San Francisco: Jossey-Bass.

Conger, J. A., & Benjamin, B. (1999). *Building leaders: How successful companies develop the next generation.* San Francisco: Jossey-Bass.

Corbally, J., & Holmberg-Wright, K. (1980). *Identifying administrative staff needs in improving academic management.* In P. Jedamus, M. W. Peterson, & Associates (Eds.). San Francisco: Jossey-Bass.

Eckel, P., Hill, H., & Green, M. (1998). *On change: En route to transformation.* Washington, DC: American Council on Education.

Garbarro, J. J. (1985). When a new manager takes charge. *Harvard Business Review,* (May–June), 110–123.

Gardner, J. W. (1987). *Leadership development.* Washington, DC: Independent Sector.

Gergen, D. (1990). Sixty something: Part 1. *U.S.News & World Report,* April 16, 64.

Gmelch, W. H. (2000). Leadership succession: How new deans take charge and learn the job. *Journal of Leadership Studies, 7*(8), 68–87.

Gmelch, W. H. (2002). *Deans balancing acts: Education leaders and the challenges they face.* Washington, DC: AACTE Publications.

Gmelch, W. H., & Miskin, V. D. (2011). Department chair leadership skills. Madison, WI: Atwood Publishing.

Gmelch, W. H., & Parkay, F. P. (1999, April). *Becoming a department chair: Negotiating the transition from scholar to administrator.* Paper presented at American Educational Research Association Conference, Montreal, Canada.

Gmelch, W. H., Reason, R. D., Schuh, J. H., & Shelley, M. C. (2002). *The call for academic leaders: The Academic Leadership Forum Report.* Ames, IA: Research Institute for Studies in Education.

Gmelch, W. H., & Seedorf, R. (1989). Academic leadership under siege: The ambiguity and imbalance of department chairs. *Journal for Higher Education Management, 5,* 37–44.

Gould, R. L. (1978). *Transformations: Growth and change in adult life.* New York: Simon & Schuster.

Hart, A. W. (1993). Leader succession and socialization: A synthesis. *Review of Educational Research, 61*(4), 451–474.

Helgesen, S. (1990). *The web of inclusion.* New York: Currency-Doubleday.

Hodgkinson, H. (2002). Demographics and teacher education—An overview. *Journal of Teacher Education, 53*(2), 102–105.

Jackson, J. F. L. (2002). Executive behavior patterns of academic deans. In W. H. Gmelch (Ed.). *Deans' balancing acts.* Washington, DC: American Association of Colleges for Teacher Education.

Kellogg Commission. (1999). *Returning to our roots: A learning society.* New York: National Association of State Universities and Land Grant Colleges.

Kellogg Foundation. (1999). *Building leadership capacity for the 21st century.* Battle Creek, MI: A Report from the Global Leadership Scan.

King, D. (2002). The changing shape of leadership. *Educational Leadership, 59*(8), 61–63.

Kouzes, J. M., & Posner, B. Z. (1987). *The leadership challenge: How to get extraordinary things done in organizations.* San Francisco: Jossey-Bass.

Kouzes, J. M., & Posner, B. Z. (2006). *A leader's legacy.* San Francisco: Jossey-Bass.

Levinson, D. J. (1978). *The seasons of a man's life.* New York: Knopf.

Louis, M. R. (1980). Surprise and sense making: What newcomers experience in entering unfamiliar organizational settings. *Administrative Science Quarterly, 25,* 226–251.

MacPherson, R. H. S. (1984). On being and becoming an educational administrator: Some methodological issues. *Educational Administration Quarterly, 20,* 58–75.

Matusak, L. R. (1997). *Finding your voice: Learning to lead . . . Anywhere you want to make a difference.* San Francisco: Jossey-Bass.

Mintzberg, H. (1973). *The nature of managerial work.* New York: Harper & Row.

Morgan, G. (1980). Paradigms, metaphors and puzzle solving in organizational theory. *Administrative Science Quarterly, 16,* 607–622.

O'Reilly, B. (1994, August 8). What's killing the business school deans of America. *Fortune,* 64–68.

Ortiz, F. I. (1982). *Career patterns in education.* New York: Praeger.

Schon, D. A. (1983). *The reflective practitioner: How professionals think in action.* New York: Basic Books.

Seedorf, R. (1990). *Transition to leadership: The university department chair.* Doctoral dissertation: Washington State University, Pullman.

Sheehy, G. (1976). *Passages: Predictable crises of adult life.* New York: Dutton.

Sheehy, G. (1995). *New passages: Mapping your life across time.* New York: Random House.

Sorenson, G. J. (2000). Taking robes off: When leaders step down. In B. Kellerman & L. R. Matusak (Eds.), *Cutting edge: Leadership 2000* (137–141). College Park, MD: Center for the Advanced Study of Leadership.

Staton-Spicer, A. Q., & Spicer, H. H. (1987). Socialization of academic chairperson: A typology of communication dimensions. *Educational Administration Quarterly, 23*(1), 41–64.

van Gennep, A. (1960). *Rites of passage* (M. B. Vizedom & G. L. Chaffee, trans). Chicago: University of Chicago Press.

Wolverton, M., & Gmelch, W. H. (2002). *College deans: Leading from within.* Westwood, CT: Oryx Press.

2

SPRINGTIME OF
A DEAN'S CAREER

In nature, spring is the season of new growth. Blue skies, sun, and warm air foster this growth. But spring is also the season of storms—heavy rain and wind occasionally accompanied by hail or tornados. And so it is with spring deans, those in their first three years of service. Like Mother Nature, the deans of spring are primed to foster growth in their colleges, but this growth doesn't always come easily; in fact, it is sometimes quite difficult. This growth, however, provides lessons spring deans want to share.

Getting Started: The First Three Years

We don't generally hear the voices of those who are new to the deanship; rather, we focus on the advice of old-hands, those who have been around for some time. But there is a lot to be learned from those in the first season of a deanship, issues and experiences that many of us have forgotten. Among the experiences unique to those in the springtime of their deanship are the reasons they initially decided to even consider trying their hand at being a dean, and from there, the processes they used in preparation for interviewing and getting ready to walk in the door of a new college.

This chapter probes those aspects of the deanship that gave these individuals a deep sense of satisfaction and accomplishment. Not surprisingly, because a dean is the focus of much that goes on in a college, the spring deans also had experiences that left them feeling dissatisfied. And, for several, one of the least considered issues they had to deal with as a dean was the extent of tension that unexpectedly existed between their professional role and their personal obligations. Suddenly, not having control over their own calendar took on new meaning. And lastly, the springtime deans interviewed for this study describe the position of a dean from their new perspective. They also have some advice to share with others considering seeking a deanship.

Preparing for the Deanship

Professors customarily enter higher education to engage in scholarship and teach in their discipline. So it is not surprising that none of the spring deans started their professional life planning on becoming deans. Some were nominated for positions and others made the decision themselves to apply. Regardless of the route they took, they all shared some common experiences before getting to the application stage.

Each of the spring deans had extensive administrative experience as a faculty member. They chaired significant college-wide and university-wide committees, served time as a department chair, headed up a major college initiative, or held leadership roles in professional associations. In fact, many of the spring deans had done all of this and more. In these positions, they had gained a perspective on the university as a whole; their thinking extended beyond the confines of their own programs and colleges. One spring dean's advice to those thinking of applying for a deanship was "become familiar with all of the academic programs in your college, look at the big picture, and get a perspective on the university level." In fact, the university-wide experience turned out to be seminal for many deans: "It gave me a broader perspective of the university." As another dean said, "It is important to have an across-campus perspective. You have to have a sense of what a university is and how it functions rather than just a department or college. While all institutions have their own way of doing things, the same things need to be handled on each campus."

Regardless of the shape or content of their administrative experiences, all of the spring deans we interviewed had served in a variety of leadership roles and been recognized for them. A traditional route to the deanship used to be a progression from program chair to department chair to assistant or associate dean. Although some still follow this trajectory, it is just as common for deans to obtain administrative experience in a wide variety of ways. One dean said, "I chaired a committee and did it well, and so I was given additional responsibilities and did them well. This pattern just kept repeating until I decided to try another position." Over their faculty careers, the deans began to see themselves, and be seen by others, as people who could be trusted to get something done. A number of those interviewed indicated that as faculty members, they had been encouraged by their dean or someone in central administration to take on additional administrative positions. Not all of the spring deans experienced support and encouragement from their institutional leaders; some found them through colleagues or self-reflection.

Once a faculty member begins to think seriously about applying for a deanship, what are the next steps? Every spring dean interviewed began the same way. They all did their homework by reading about educational issues at the national level. One dean summarized it this way: "When I began to seriously consider applying for the deanship, I began to read widely and deeply the literature on education at the national level; what was going on, what was important. I felt I had to know about the national discussion around teacher education. I began to think about education in a larger picture than just my field." And yet another dean summed up this point by saying, "You can no longer be parochial in terms of interests." This common response led many to pore over professional publications such as *The Chronicle of Higher Education* and *Kappan* and explore websites dedicated to educational issues. Others asked trusted colleagues to recommend articles and books to add to their reading list. Regardless of approach, every single dean began his or her search by first immersing himself or herself in literature on public education.

Although there appears to be a commonality regarding the experiences spring deans had that led them to believe they were qualified to apply for dean positions and how they prepared for interviews, the answers to "why" they wanted these positions and "what they thought they could contribute" are varied. As one spring dean responded, "What interested me about being a dean? It was the ability to create change." This dean went on to say, "I think I'm a good leader, and I thought I could move things." Creating change was a theme that ran through every interview with deans in their first three years. Additionally, one added, "I enjoy the hustle and bustle of administration. You meet a new challenge every day. And I like meeting people."

The experiences of all of the springtime deans we interviewed can be summarized as follows (a) university administration was not an early career plan for them; (b) they all had held leadership roles in their colleges; (c) they all had served on university-wide committees; (d) they all had received positive feedback on their leadership skills, especially from significant individuals; and (e) they began to look at their college and university through a broader, national lens.

The Search Process

In preparation for airport or campus interviews, spring deans did all they could to familiarize themselves beforehand. They delved into college web pages and read promotional materials. As one spring dean explained, "When I walked into the room, I 'knew' everyone at the table except for one young man. I had looked up the entire search committee on the web, had a copy of their picture in my briefcase, and was aware of their area of specialization. The only person I could not identify was the student representative." Another commented, "I looked up information on the university to determine something about their values to see if they would be a good fit with my own values." There is a cautionary tale here. The only dean who wasn't totally satisfied with her choice of institution said, "I have the skills my college needs to move forward, but my campus doesn't value education at all from the top down. I have no institutional support or recognition." In other words, there wasn't a "good fit" between how she envisioned her job and what she hoped to accomplish and what upper administration viewed as worthy of their support or value. Another dean approached the "fit" issue more directly. She said, "I asked the university to send me some information. In part, this was to see what they would send; I wanted to see what they thought was of value for me to see and peruse. I also explored their website and talked to their alumni."

Another dean who found himself a "missed fit" at his institution said he hadn't known the right questions to ask before accepting his position. This is where those who are moving from one deanship to another have an edge. Unfortunately, spring deans brand new to the position seldom move until later in their careers. Several spring deans did offer the advice, however, that someone attempting to land a deanship should talk to a sitting dean if possible and see what questions he or she suggests.

Once the decision to apply for a deanship was made, one individual said, "I decided *not* to apply for the position in my home institution, because

I didn't think it was a good fit for me. I really wanted to move from a master's granting university to a research one." Another spring dean elaborated:

> If you are going to apply for a deanship, you need to do a lot of prep. First you need to read carefully the university and college's website. Look for other articles about them. Ask other faculty or colleagues in your network what they know about the different institutions you are interested in. You need to spend some time deciding if there is a potential "good fit" for you on the campus. For instance, do you want to go to a research university or a regional master's degree institution? Do you have a preference for one part of the country or another; is size a consideration?

The whole search process was a new experience for the spring deans. When asked to describe how they handled it, one dean zeroed in on how he decided to which institutions to apply. His criteria were (a) national reputation in the field of education; (b) university leadership that said education was important on campus; (c) education had to be high on the agenda of the provost, if not the president; and (d) an institution that had doctoral programs and was located in the Midwest. Location was a factor for another dean, who commented, "Most of my professional career has been in another part of the country, but I have family in this area and decided it would be nice to be closer to them." Once the spring deans had explored what they desired in a deanship, several began a waiting game. The process of finding the right position often takes time. One dean related that he had applied for 3 or 4 positions per year, and probably 10 to 12 overall before he found a dean position that was a good fit. Although his search process might have been shortened if he had spent more time investigating the various universities before he applied, it might also have been the case that the information he obtained wasn't detailed enough for him to make any distinction. More likely, however, was the observation made by another dean. She shared, "I wasn't very skilled early in my search and ended up interviewing at institutions for which I wasn't a good fit. On the other hand, this gave me lots of experience making presentations to faculties and preparing me for the types of questions I would be asked. In retrospect, it was a good investment of my time."

Another dean reflected on his search, "There were some universities I didn't apply to because it was so obvious they needed someone more seasoned and experienced than me. After talking to colleagues who were there,

I uncovered major problems within the faculty that I didn't feel I had the experience to address."

Perspectives on the Deanship

We began this chapter on deans within their first three years with a discussion on why they considered applying for deanships and then how they prepared for the search process. Moving into the present, we asked them to describe what it was like to be a dean and, now that they were on the job, how they would describe the position to someone else.

The first thing new deans commented on was the amount of time the position consumes. Many had not anticipated the number of weekends and countless evenings they would spend at the office or on the job entertaining donors and attending celebrations, speeches, commencements, receptions, sporting events, and other university affairs. One of the deans summarized his new life by saying with great emphasis, "It is just a totally different world than being a faculty member!" He went on, "Faculty members work weekends and evenings too, but they have the luxury of deciding when and for how long. I never appreciated the freedom I had as a faculty member." Spring deans also bemoaned the limited control they had over their calendars. They expressed mounting frustration over their inability to get everything done—even though it felt like they spent "every waking moment" on the job. One commented, "My advice to someone interested in being a dean? It's the best job I've ever had, but, for you to work as hard as you will have to as a dean, you better love the job!"

The new deans quickly realized that the dean's office is where all the college problems finally end up. In fact, all of them commented on how much time they spent dealing with people, including faculty, staff, students, and parents. And this was just within the college. Time was also spent responding to requests from central administration and preparing materials for them and other groups. On a daily basis, deans receive bursts of information requiring them to make quick decisions, frequently about politically charged issues. They found the constant arrival of multiple issues on their desk all at once disconcerting. "I'm trying to learn to multitask, because if I don't become more efficient with my time, I'm not going to make it." One joked, "Have you seen that TV show about people who hoard things and are covered over with old magazines and used soda pop cans? I keep thinking the show's camera crew is going to show up at my office door. It's been a month since I've seen the top of my desk." Several added that if "you are the type of person who prefers to begin one task at a time, complete it, and then move on, then being a dean isn't for you."

Early in their tenure, the spring deans began putting together a well-functioning leadership team. Within our sample, those externally selected tended to keep existing associate and assistant deans and department chairs for at least a year as they eased into their new position. However, after learning local culture and the personalities, some made personnel changes. This wasn't always easy. Each of the individuals being replaced had the support of friends and colleagues who weren't aware of the ways in which they weren't being effective or were even undermining the dean. One female dean reported that early in her tenure she decided to move the college-wide copy machine from her office to the technology center. A male department chair looked at her and said, "Who gave you the authority to make that change?" He didn't remain a chair for long.

For some deans, an unexpected aspect of the position was the press to become engaged with national educational issues and the necessity to get to know all the players, including the staff in the state department of education, local state representatives, and Congressional representatives and senators. Regular visits to the state capital and Washington, D.C., were also unanticipated aspects of the position. The spring deans, although intensely involved with their colleges and campuses, had not appreciated how involved they would have to become within the political realm. Most embraced this aspect of the position and found it exciting. "I like being able to influence the policy makers on issues impacting education. It makes me feel good that my views are respected and that those in a position of authority who are able to make change truly listen to what I have to say." "As dean, you get to participate in creating a vision that transcends your own discipline or unit. That's exhilarating." "I like being a stakeholder in the whole university. As dean, I get to participate in the life of the institution, well beyond one college."

None of the spring deans interviewed regretted their decision to become a dean. Although they didn't like some aspects, on the whole they felt it was a great job. And all answered in the affirmative when asked, "If you could do it over again, would you become a dean?" One went on to add, "Universities need good leaders. I know how important the job is and I believe I'm good at it."

With a little probing, the deans described what they loved best about their new positions. At the top of the list was the satisfaction they got from working with faculty and staff to move the school, college, and department of education forward. They liked building programs and representing their college to the rest of the campus and the community. Several indicated that being dean allowed them to be much more creative than they had assumed possible. They loved it. They liked building strong programs and mentoring faculty. They also "liked the challenges and thrived on them." Seeing and planning the big picture was mentioned as a plus. "I like looking down the road seeing where I would like the college to go." One dean even "enjoyed the fund raising and participation with colleague deans on the campus level to create an improved university." Another commented, "I like moving education (this college) forward in terms of improving the quality of the teachers we prepare."

A sense of commitment also pervaded the spring deans' comments. Many vowed they were "here to serve the college." One dean added, "The job is more than just understanding the budget and policies. It really is about relational skills and interacting with people. That's what you spend most of your day doing. You have to have those people skills, and you've got to be out there interacting with the people."

Although spring deans felt their highest satisfaction was derived from working with people, it also was the area that gave them their highest levels of dissatisfaction. Many of the deans talked about dealing with negative faculty. Although often just an irritant or something simple to be dealt with, one dean described a more serious issue. He had a group of senior faculty who were opposed to any change. "But, of course, I had been brought in to bring about change, so I was the target." He ultimately had to get support from central administration. Working with faculty or staff is not always pleasant, but it does come with the position. Because any significant personnel issue in a college ends up on the dean's desk, the person in the role has to be able to deal with it.

After personnel issues, the most frequently cited issue the deans we interviewed found challenging was dealing with tough budget situations. Many of them walked into their positions with high expectations as to what they would be able to accomplish to move their colleges forward. Instead, they were greeted by a steadily decreasing budget with which to reach those expectations. Another problematic issue was having to deal with central administration or other deans and faculty on campus who had a low opinion of their college and its programs. Some felt they weren't given any respect and were treated like second-class citizens. One dean attributed her inability to move the college forward to the perceptions of the college held by central administration. "I have the skills to do what needs to be done, but not the support."

Another problematic issue for several was being micromanaged by central administration or by someone on an oversight board. "Everything I do is scrutinized and has to be approved at every level. I feel like I'm being squashed under central administration's collective thumb, and it sure hasn't done much for my ability to create new programs or explore new ventures."

Spring deans also found it difficult to deal with time pressures. "You have no control over your own time in the deanship. I've adjusted to this, but it wasn't easy—and I still don't like it." Several mentioned that, initially, they found it difficult to decide which campus events they had to attend and which ones they could skip. "During September and October, I don't think I had one complete weekend at home. I am forcing myself to learn how to manage my calendar because, if I don't, I'll never have any personal time." "Blocking out time for myself is a big deal. I'm not good at doing it yet but I'm working on it."

Several stressed their desire to have a personal life as well as a professional one; the deanship had caused the two to sometimes be in conflict. "All working couples have to figure out how to deal with the multiple tasks of everyday life, but when I suddenly became a dean, it was a real transition for my partner." There are endless numbers of events to which deans and their spouses or partners are invited. But it doesn't take long for the non-dean to realize that for most of these there is no real role for them.

A few spring deans talked about the new division of labor within their family unit. Their spouse or partner found himself or herself picking up all the tasks that used to be shared. "I don't have time anymore to do the laundry, go to the grocery store, or stay home for the plumber. My husband has taken on these essential responsibilities." Several female deans felt that this shift in duties had put a strain on their relationship with their spouse or partner, especially those who were asked to suborn his or her own profession or personal activities. Some dean couples handled this change in roles easily, but others found it created tensions that had to be faced.

One of the female deans mentioned another adjustment: "The whole guy-spouse thing. My husband has had to learn to watch what he says in public. It's been hard for him because his role at public events now is as my spouse, and this is different. Also his last name isn't the same as mine, but we still show up at places where they put my last name on his name tag."

Two deans new to the role commented that they were very private individuals. One continued, "There are days when I spend all day talking to people and when I get home I don't want to talk at all, but my husband has been waiting all day to talk to me. So I have to push myself into being a companion."

The deans we interviewed in their first three years in the role described the steep learning curve they had learned to navigate. By the second year, most were well aware of the demands their positions placed on them and their families. They were frequently stressed. Yet at the end of the day, none of them regret the decision to become a dean. They find deep satisfaction in the role and most report that it is the best job they have ever had.

3

SUMMERTIME OF
A DEAN'S CAREER

Hitting Your Stride: Years Four to Seven

Years four through seven, the summer of a dean's career, find established deans reaping the benefits of their earlier labors. It is a time of fulfillment, the season when deans finally see their hard work nurturing the college environment, planting ideas, and cultivating collaboration, showing constructive growth and the promise of full bloom. Programmatic ideas they sowed three years ago have taken root and, in turn, are germinating other new and creative ideas. Healthy expansion and the promise of even greater program and enrollment growth in the future have become realities. Summer deans are more aware of how to do things and have become more comfortable with the deanship—and with being dean. The painful beginnings they experienced in the springtime of their deanships are, hopefully, over.

Unfortunately, the honeymoon is over as well. Many of the changes that needed to be made in the college have been or are occurring, and the dean is the one held responsible—especially if the changes have been unpopular. By the fourth and fifth years, summer deans have built their leadership teams, and their colleges, overall, should finally be coming together. Those faculty and staff who were not contributing to the institution or found the dean's leadership style distracting have, hopefully, found academic homes elsewhere. Many of the early goals that summer deans shared with their faculty and staff are nearing fruition; others hold promise because the team is working together. Is the fifth year best? Does the job become easier with time? Are the deans who find themselves midstride in the deanship more effective, or do they lose momentum the longer they serve?

Journey Into the Deanship

In this study, the deans in the summer of their career averaged five years on the job and the majority were still in their first deanship. It is interesting to note that many of the deans interviewed believed that they "fell into the position" by "being in the right place at the right time." One commented that he not only fell into the position, he almost drowned. While chair of educational administration, one of the largest graduate departments on his campus, he was flattered when asked by upper administration to become dean of a new, blended college that folded the previous education, consumer science, and health professions colleges and schools into one. He commented that his longtime relationship with the provost, who happened to be a member of the same educational administration department previous to his own appointment, was probably a major factor in his being asked to serve. He also volunteered that being a close friend of the provost had been a hindrance and a help. What this dean found most difficult was that it took well into the summer of his deanship for faculty to accept him as qualified—even though a number of them had accepted his leadership as their chair previous to his appointment as dean. During his first years in the role, the faculty members were so angry with the way in which he had been appointed that they could not bring themselves to accept any of his ideas as feasible—even when they knew their college would benefit. "Six years into it, things are better now," he commented, "but I wouldn't recommend my route to the deanship for anyone, and, if I had been wiser, I would have turned it down regardless of how much I was tempted."

Another dean who had been the associate dean for several years experienced a different reaction to her appointment. When the dean she worked for retired, the decision was made to waive a national search, and she was appointed from within. In this case, unlike the appointed dean mentioned previously, the new in-house "dean" felt that she had the backing of the faculty immediately. Overall, the deans, several of whom were appointed or selected from within, felt that this was not the preferred route to the deanship. They also felt that being the internal candidate or selectee was more often a hardship than a help.

Satisfactions and Dissatisfactions

Not every summer dean was selected internally. A number of those interviewed had made a more conscious choice to attain the deanship. One shared that over a two-year period, he had applied for 27 dean positions before he was selected to lead a college of education at a major Research I institution. His ultimate goal was to become a provost, and he had allotted himself a specific number of years in the deanship before moving on.

Another felt fortunate that her first invitation to a state university as a finalist resulted in a deanship. However, she expressed remorse that she had not been aware of the unspoken leadership parameters that institutions follow but do not always share. "I did not realize how difficult it will be for me to return to a private institution now that I have served as dean of a public institution for the past seven years," she lamented. "My ultimate goal is to preside over a small private liberal arts institution. Instead, I may never find a position outside of the public higher education sector." Historically, a great many private institutions—because fundraising skill is so vital for their administrators—seek candidates from other private universities and colleges rather than those with public higher education experience. However, because of the number of state-supported institutions that find their financial backing by the state eroding and lacking, this practice may change. Today, public institution deans find themselves on the road, building their donor base, as often as their private institution colleagues.

Overall, this group of summer deans felt that it had taken them two to four years to really feel comfortable in the job. One dean said she felt so uptight for the first couple of years "that I questioned if I shouldn't return to the faculty." She went on to explain, "Finally, after four-plus years on the job, I found myself settling in to the role. Do you know I didn't even hang any pictures in my office for the first three years? I kept telling myself it was because I was too busy. Looking back, more likely it was because I wanted to make a quick getaway if I had to."

Most summer deans felt that they hit their stride when they were "making changes, not just learning acronyms," "when faculty accepted me," and "when I felt safe enough to take a risk." Being knowledgeable of the many unique programs in the college and all of the people made a big difference in the comfort level for many of those who were interviewed. "It took me a long time to understand the structure of all of our programs," one commented, "but, once I did, I felt like I could do my job better—and easier." Another pointed out, "My background is educational administration, but, as dean, I have to speak to—and sell when it comes to potential donors—all of our programs. It was important for me to understand audiology and kinesiology as well as I understand how to prepare individuals to become principals."

Several commented that building relationships with legislators, donors, other deans, and administrators, as well as with members of the community, took hours of their time and attention. "Now that I've been on the job long enough to know who's who, I can make my way through receptions, greet the movers and the shakers, and still get home before the news at eleven. During my first few years, working the crowd was impossible. I just didn't have the connections."

Relationships take time. Over and over again, the summer deans noted how much their years of experience had impacted positively their friend-raising and fundraising capabilities. They pointed out that before they had an awareness of specific individuals and their importance to the college, whether it was an alum, a donor, or a business partner, it felt like they were trying to move the college's initiatives forward with one hand tied behind their back. As one summer dean so aptly stated, "I could never have accomplished the gains we made during this past capital campaign when I was new to this job. The first three years, I didn't even have a clue as to who I should be inviting to our tailgates. For that matter, it has taken me six years just to be recognized by name when I show up at Rotary."

During this season of their career, summer deans felt they received their greatest satisfaction from people. The other campus deans were friends now, and cross-campus collaborations were a lot easier to initiate and move along. No longer the "new dean" at the provost's table, summer deans expressed more satisfaction in their interactions with fellow deans and upper administration and felt more comfortable in making comments and suggestions. "My first two years as a dean, I never opened my mouth at the Dean's Council. I was afraid I'd say something stupid or ask a question that every dean ought to know, so I just kept my mouth shut—even when my head was spinning with questions that I wished were answered," one commented.

Several summer deans mentioned that working with faculty had become easier and a lot more rewarding over the years. One shared, "To be honest, I was afraid of the faculty my first few years. I knew they opposed some of the changes I had been charged to complete when I was hired, and there were times when I felt like a bulletproof vest wasn't a bad idea." Another commented, "Now that the faculty are used to me and my leadership style, I think we work better together. It's like we all know one another's hot buttons now and try not to punch them too often." Yet another commented, "Our college is like a family . . . the more we work together and support one another, the stronger we've become. And now that a couple of our crankiest members finally decided to retire and moved to Alabama, we are all a lot happier. Both kept the dissention pot boiling."

The pleasure many summer deans find in their interactions with people may be, in part, a result of time on the job.

> My interactions with students are what I really look forward to each day— especially when they don't relate to a problem. Now that I've been the dean for a number of years, I feel like I've heard it all! Even though I know that's not true, I am aware that my experience comes into play when I'm faced with a student problem or dilemma. I don't come right out and say "been there, done that," but I do catch myself smiling on the inside as I listen to someone's "new" problem.

Ironically, personnel issues also caused summer deans their greatest dissatisfaction. Several mentioned the pettiness of faculty and staff. "At times our secretarial staff reminds me of fourth grade girls on the playground— unwilling to work together and constantly sniping at one another." One commented, "I will never figure out why faculty in one department would rather watch the demise of their own programs than collaborate with another department to make all of their programs more viable." Several summer deans said that the jealousy among their faculty members always took them by surprise, regardless of their years as dean. One shared, "I never expect it from individuals who are supposed to be so smart."

Several were also disheartened by the faculty's disinterest in students. As one summer dean put it, "I have some faculty members who are downright mean. I'm not even sure what attracted them to the teaching profession in the first place because they certainly don't care for students." The summer deans found their need to remind faculty about posting office hours, attending graduation ceremonies, participating in college events, and so on, a tedious but necessary chore. "Some gripe that I won't approve them for tenure if they don't go to the end of the school year picnic. That isn't true but there are days when I'm tempted."

Dealing With Difficult Issues

The personnel issues causing the greatest concern for deans at this point in their deanship centered on promotion, tenure, and termination decisions.

Never easy, the summer deans did express that, through the years, they had developed more confidence in making the hard calls. "I used to get migraines writing letters of nonsupport. I still find it one of the hardest parts of my job—but, I am more comfortable saying 'no.'" Several pointed out that they had learned the hard way not to be too lenient in giving individuals another chance. "Every time I try to be the nice guy, it comes back and bites me." "The longer I am in the deanship, the easier it is to evaluate—really evaluate regardless of whether it is a grant proposal approval or a tenure decision. Now if I could just convince my chairs to do likewise."

There also are the people who, as one dean expressed, "drive me up the wall." Several of the summer deans commented that the longer they serve as deans the less patience they have. "I think I've learned to be a better listener, but I have less tolerance for some of the inane requests people have." "Years ago, I had an open-door policy and took it upon myself to get intimately involved in every little problem the college had. No more. I've learned to trust my chairs and work hard not to let anyone do inroads around them." This sentiment was shared by many.

When necessary, however, the summer deans seemed comfortable addressing difficult issues head-on and recognized that, as deans, the buck did stop with them. One voiced professional, and personal, satisfaction that she had handled several sexual harassment charges promptly and appropriately. "Over the last six years, I have learned that university procedures and policies are there for a reason and when it comes to cases of harassment—of any type—I follow them step by step," she said. "When I have a really sticky problem—like a male faculty member making inappropriate suggestive comments to young women in his class, for instance—I deal with it immediately." Added another, "Problems of this type don't get any easier and putting them off sometimes makes it worse. That's one thing I've learned through the years—take care of the messy stuff immediately." One nodded and said, "My EEO officer is on speed dial."

Several of the summer deans inherited colleges in which instances of harassment, plagiarism, and an unhealthy work environment, among other issues, were routinely ignored. "When I accepted my second deanship, I discovered that the college had been misappropriating student fees for years. Luckily, I had a similar issue in my first deanship and, even though it is never easy handling something of this magnitude, having dealt with it previously sure did help."

Several summer deans mentioned that the longer they held the dean's position the more receptive they were to the suggestions of others. They found the job easier and more rewarding once they realized the value of "give-and-take." As one dean aptly stated, "I used to see everything as black or white; in reality, I deal with a whole lot of gray." Another summer dean reflected, "I'm not as 'my way or the highway' as I used to be. There are a whole slew of good ways to do most things—and most of them don't happen to be mine."

An example one dean gave related to college structure: "Although I still feel we could function more effectively and save financially as three large departments rather than seven small ones, I have learned to live with the structure we have. That decision, by the way, is a direct result of my years on the job." He continued, "As a brand new dean, I can't tell you how many times I was tempted to switch everything around, but, through the years, I've learned to save my ammunition for the really big fights. Reshuffling our departments, with all of the necessary program and personnel realignments, would cause as much angst among our faculty as who gets the office with the window. I found out a long time ago that the efficiency we might gain by restructuring isn't worth the hard feelings a move of this type would generate."

This observation was shared by several of the summer deans who commented that, unless some "extenuating circumstances" called for a shake-up in structure, they had learned to live with what they had. One dean said, "As long as classes are getting scheduled; curricula are being discussed, revised, and created; and evaluations are being conducted, I figure, 'if it ain't broke, don't fix it.'"

Adaptability, a trait that many of the summer deans appear to have perfected, serves them well when it comes to their relationships with upper administration—especially when so many presidents and provosts are short-timers. In numerous instances, the summer deans felt that upper administration was a "moving target." Most summer deans have experienced at least one change in the presidency and two or more in the provost position. One dean in his seventh year expressed his frustration: "I've had four presidents and five provosts since accepting the deanship." He continued, "It wouldn't be so bad if they all came in to the university with the same mind-set, but they don't. Every president wants to make his or her mark, and what they want to accomplish is as varied as who they are and where they come from.

Don't even get me started on the provosts. Now with my fifth, I'm having to, once again, educate her about education—just like the four before her. Previously a dean of science and technology, she has no idea about pre-K–12 education, how it works, and how it impacts on our programs."

This continual shifting of upper administration has, in some instances, led to changes in the deanship as well. Summer deans realize that unless their personal and college goals are compatible with those of the provost and president, it is probably time to dust off the vitae and begin applying for the next position, whether another deanship, a provost spot, or a presidency. With substantial dean experience, those in the summer of their career, years four through seven, often find themselves sought after by search committees and professional headhunters. The dilemma, however, is whether or not to go, especially when there is no guarantee that the next position will be any more stable. For several deans these professional decisions, like staying or leaving, were influenced by other more personal factors. Some at this stage of their lives found that care for elderly parents prohibited relocation to another position. Others commented that they were uncomfortable uprooting their children. Still others chose to stay in their present positions because of the economy, housing costs, the fear of not being able to sell a home, and a spouse's job, among others.

Overall, the deans who were in the summer of their career enjoyed "making things happen." They were proud of their accomplishments: developing new programs, receiving accreditation for current programs, creating new research centers, and changing a "long overdue" college climate. When they "hit their stride," they still enjoyed deaning—most of the time—but realized that it did not get any easier. Their comfort came from knowing what to do, but they realized they had more to do. Associate deans and spouses provided support, but their lives had not become any less complicated through the years.

What is next for deans who have reached this point in their career? Staying put? Consulting? Returning to the faculty? Seeking a provost position or a presidency? Now that they have "hit their stride," can they keep the fire alive in their current deanship? The next group of deans shed some light on these questions.

4

FALL OF A DEAN'S CAREER

Keeping the Fire Alive: Eight Years and Beyond

Not all deans entered the fall season of harvest of the deanship, because many changed jobs, changed professions, or moved into retirement. For many others who stayed in the deanship, the fall season is a time of reduced growth, when things slow down, weariness starts to set in, and hot weather wanes along with enthusiasm. However, the early harvest and attention to the culture and climate does bear fruit. Everyone knows the dean well. The institution relies on his or her stability. In many instances, the experienced dean has lasted longer than several presidents and provosts. But for most seasoned deans, the fall represents a period of plateau. They need something new to continue their growth. Attention is paid to new goals and learning new things, or they will die on the vine, go to seed. How does the dean at this season of life keep boredom from creeping in, or is it even an issue? How do deans keep focused on what is truly important and sustainable (Hargreaves & Fink, 2006)? How many deans at this stage of life are waiting for retirement? How many have aspirations of going higher in academe? In the fall of the deanship, how does the dean stay focused and keep the fire alive?

What is next for the fall deans who have hit their stride? The fall deans' responses were as varied as staying put in their present position, consulting or returning to the faculty, or seeking a provost position or presidency. Once deans hit their stride, how long can they keep the fire alive in their current deanship? The fall deans shed some light on this question.

Dean Loop: Zoom or Doom?

Staying in the deanship too long can result in losing interest in the job, failing to keep up with changes in the field, and possibly entering a performance plateau—a dean doom loop (Gmelch, Damico, Hopkins, & Mitchell, 2009; Hollander, 1991), as portrayed in Figure 4.1.

New deans enter quadrant I in their springtime, with a steep learning curve as they learn new skills and find new interests. Note the learning curve is not a straight line. Deans learn and move up the learning curve only when they experiment and experience new challenges. The real issue for deans is not how fast they can learn, but how quickly they can learn from their mistakes (see Kouzes & Posner, 2006, p. 167). One noted anthropologist who had also been a dean at one time observed that learning to be a dean is

FIGURE 4.1
The Dean Loop "Zoom to Doom"

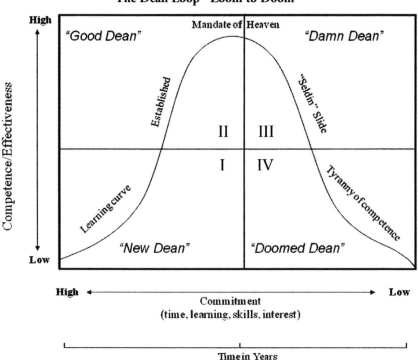

like learning to ice-skate in front of your faculty. Although all deans experienced failures and disappointments, they observed how to handle their goofs over time, which ultimately determined their success and effectiveness.

The "new deans" progress to the "good deans" in late spring and summer as they become committed to the position and competent in their duties (quadrant II). The confident deans, now in quadrant II, are careful not to go over the edge and down the slide to becoming a "damn dean" (quadrant III) or a "doomed dean" (quadrant IV). Many deans talked about knowing when it is time to go. A university leader and noted historian-scholar referred to an ancient Chinese concept called the "mandate of heaven"—a time when it was the followers' duty or calling to relieve the ruler. "It's the 15% rule," remarked a fall dean. "You can continue until 15% of your faculty oppose you." Others felt when they lost 51% of their faculty, it was time to get out of Dodge! A reflective, visionary dean's strategy was to leave a year or two before he approached the plateau. He didn't want to hit the "Seldin Slide," named after a dean colleague who served eight years but admitted he should have left after six.

Those staying too long often are tagged as the "damn dean" (quadrant III). And those remaining past the bountiful harvest go to seed and experience the "tyranny of competence" and are doomed—quadrant IV. Over the years, they learned the technical aspects of being a dean and speak eloquently about campus issues and national trends, but they have lost the zest to be effective. As Barry Posner, former dean at the University of Santa Clara, posits, "Any leadership practice can become destructive. Virtues can become vices. Strengths can become weaknesses" (Kouzes & Posner, 2006, p. 172).

How many years does this Zoom to Doom curve represent? Where is the midpoint? How many years before the "mandate of heaven" sets in and the faculty feel it is time for a dean to move on? How long before a dean voluntarily or psychologically feels like the energy and excitement are waning? Although each dean had his or her personalized dean loop in terms of years, one dean summed it up: "For six years I was highly motivated, the seventh year I felt it dwindling, and by the eighth year it was time to make a change." Just being competent was not enough for many fall deans to keep the fire alive.

Extending the Dean's Fall Season

The keys to all long-serving fall deans rested in continuous learning and energizing change. Fall deans spoke of being reinvigorated through (a) changing the **content** of the current deanship (e.g., new emphases, new priorities, new people, new frame of leadership), or (b) changing the **context** by taking on a new deanship. Fall deans saw their careers as being either *between* multiple deanships and institutions (protean deans) or *within* a single deanship (institutional deans).

Protean Deans: Career Between Multiple Deanships

The *protean deans* experienced their career as one without boundaries by going through stages of exploration, establishment, and mastery (Arthur & Fousseau, 1996) within one deanship and then shifting to another deanship, and possibly another. Many entered the deanship "by accident," being asked to serve as the interim dean when a vacancy opened late in the year without time to launch a national search. Although this "accidental" dean may feel loyalty and commitment to compete to become the "real" dean, many explore possibilities outside their institution to test the waters of their marketability and to "see what's out there." After serving in their first deanship for a few years, some deans experienced the "five- or seven-year itch" and needed to make a move to a more prestigious institution, a new set of institutional challenges, or a different type of institution (public to private). They see their deanship as more cosmopolitan (across institutions) than local (within an institution).

Institutional Deans: Career Within One Deanship

Whereas protean deans kept their fire alive by changing institutions, *institutional deans* stoked their fires within one institution. Deans, on average, serve six years. A dean in her 15th year at one institution said she really had three deanships within one. "When you have been in a deanship for a long period of time, you recognize that the job changes. Some lose their enthusiasm when they see what they've been doing isn't working. On the other hand, you can't help but get enthusiastic about deciding the next place you want your college to be."

In addition to the changing nature of the deanship, another dean reflected, "One of the worst times for me was when a new academic vice president-provost was really mucking up the works, and I figured I was going to lose and didn't want to work under those conditions, but he left, so I stayed." Another impetus for sustaining long-serving deans comes when the faculty scenery changes:

> While my deanly duties haven't changed significantly over the years, the cast of players has. The first few years of my deanship, I dreaded going to the office as three quarters of my faculty had been there a quarter of a century and were recalcitrant, myopic, and change phobic. Now, six years later, I have 40 percent new faculty, and I love going to work to help them grow and get tenured. I live for my faculty, their enthusiasm, and fresh spirit and *can do* attitude they bring to the college.

How Deans Plateau

None of the fall deans in this study had started down the Seldin Slide. They found ways to experience the fall colors within their current deanship or by changing to a new dean position at another institution. However, all of the fall deans experienced feeling that they had reached a plateau at some point. The old adage of the seven-year itch rang true for many fall deans who expressed the need every six to eight years to change crops or do a little crop rotation (new faculty, new college, new institution), to place their professional field in fallow (take a sabbatical or leave to build up nutrients in the soil or their soul and reenergize their batteries), or to pull up their root stock (start a new crop in new land) and begin again. These fall deans served an average of 12 years in the deanship. One quarter served 12 years or more in a single deanship, and the other three quarters served in two or three deanships. They talked about the conditions that influenced the feeling of being on a plateau in the deanship.

Boredom From Repetition and Routine

After a few years sitting in the dean's chair, the scenery starts looking the same. The weekly or bimonthly meetings with the provost and deans address more mundane management issues than cutting-edge leadership opportunities. Budgets continue to erode, and they are forced to continually look back to cut budgets rather than ahead to advance programs. Faculty conflicts start to repeat themselves over the years; it is only the players that change. The

once intellectually stimulated dean now feels numb and dummied down by
continual "administrivia" and meaningless problem solving. Deans want to
make a difference but feel caught in the "activity trap" of management: "I
didn't realize how numb and uninspired I was intellectually until I read an
academically challenging article the other day that got me to think conceptually again. I had been living in a world of brevity, variety, and fragmentation
in my decanal work, and I missed the excitement of conceptual thinking."

Diminishing Rate of Return

Some deans felt their investment of time and energy diminished over the
years. A business dean reflected, "After eight years, I felt that I had made the
impact that I probably would be capable of making, and if I stayed for
another 4 or 5 years, the degree of impact would diminish year to year. I'd
be a caretaker." Finally, an education dean summed it up by saying that
probably 80% of the major changes in his deanship and the college occurred
in the first four years. The final years he felt he was tinkering and experienced
only incremental changes. Yet the last 20% took five, six, or eight times the
amount of effort as the first 80%. He then decided to take on another challenge: a deanship at another institution.

Slumping Learning Curve

The decline in the learning curve troubled many of the deans. They entered
the academy to be part of a learning organization. Some said being a faculty
member was the best job they could imagine. Where else are you paid to
learn? As portrayed in quadrants I and II, the deanship has a steep learning
curve but after a while the curve plateaus and the lack of intellectual stimula-
tion from the "madness of meetings" and "administrivia" becomes deafen-
ing. As a medical dean quipped, "The only difference between being dean
and being dead is one letter."

Atrophy of Academic Skills

Most deans spend more than two decades in their disciplines as doctoral
students and then move through the ranks of the professorship, department
chair, and/or associate deanship before becoming a dean.

> At least as a department chair I vowed not to have only one new line on
> my vita, *department chair,* representing the past four years of academic

productivity. I wanted to continue my publications and teaching to keep my academic fire alive while "serving" my term as chair. Being a dean is totally different. Deans are no longer rewarded for their academic productivity. In fact my provost chastises me for teaching a class, and my publications go unnoticed and unrecognized. Central administration just wants me to take care of the shop! My fiduciary responsibilities suck up my time and energy, and there is nothing left to give to my academic endeavors. Over time, I lost contact with my discipline, and I even wonder if I can ever return to the classroom again as my discipline has passed me by.

Note that only 25% of deans return to the faculty, and even department chairs are stressed about "not being able to keep up in my academic field while serving as chair" (Gmelch & Miskin, 2011; Wolverton & Gmelch, 2002). In essence, fall deans testified that their academic skills began to atrophy, and even the administrative skills they learned along the decanal path became routine and were no longer as stimulating as they had been during the learning process experienced as a new dean (quadrants I and II). In frustration, one dean lamented, "You don't ever learn the deanship!" Ultimately deans even question their ability to return to the classroom. A New York City dean recovering from quadruple bypass surgery said, "I will give it two more years as dean, but in the end, I can't return to *my theater*— teaching. Seats in my 'Broadway' private university classroom are $200 a night, and I can't produce the script they deserve after being away from 'the show' for 20 years."

Not Making a "Significant" Difference

After spending five or six years' time in the office, deans felt they were making less of a significant difference. One dean made the analogy of how his "impact curve" looked like a learning curve:

> When you start as a dean there is a lot of impact brewing, and then its line starts to flatten out and the longer you go, the more you plateau. You may have made 80% of your impact in the first five years and the question is how many more years is it worth it to nudge maybe an extra 10%? For me, it wasn't worth any more than eight years of my time.

How Deans Managed the Plateau Effect

All the deans felt they reached a plateau at some point during their deanship. Just feeling competent was not enough to keep the fire alive. Some entered what might be termed the "tyranny of competence," where they had mastered the skills of being a dean but lost the patience, zest, and passion to serve their colleagues, clients, and students. Students became numbers, and faculty represented distractions. Whereas earlier in the deans' seasons faculty created exciting challenges, now they were seen as annoyances. The deans had been there before. How many more strategic plans would they develop? What more for the faculty could they do to keep them satisfied? Had they lost the patience to deal with faculty's bickering and whining over trivial issues? With tighter budgets in tough economic times, how many more dollars must they raise from outside sources in order to placate donors' and alumnae's self-interests? Deans entered the academy to learn and advance their discipline, but after years in the deanship, many ask, "What have I learned lately? I have been away from my discipline for years—can I ever return to faculty to teach and reengage in scholarship?"

Tactics for Stoking the Fire

The length of time deans spend in their fall season, and ultimately serve in their positions, depends on their personality and goals, college needs and challenges, and changes in staff and faculty (Buller, 2007). Do fall deans still find meaning and challenge in their positions? Lev Vygotsky's theory of "the zone of proximal development" (as cited in Buller, 2007, p. 395) postulates that people learn best and have the greatest satisfaction when they are challenged to stretch their abilities but are not overwhelmingly challenged to the point of frustration and discouragement. The fall deans in our study maintained the "zone of proximal development" (quadrant II in dean loop) through a series of tactics to keep them challenged, interested, motivated, and learning. Whether deans served within one or across several institutions, they used similar techniques to keep learning and igniting their fires.

Tinker Tactics: Augment Personal Skills and Interests

Tinker tactics were used to stretch new skills and learn new ideas through new assignments, committees, commissions, team members, and faculty. Many fall deans focused on retreading challenges inside the college and institution rather than retreating to another institution. Inside their colleges, they focused on building their leadership team of associate deans and department chairs and advancing their faculty and staff to new leadership positions. One dean stated, "The real success was not about *me*, but *we*, the college leadership team. In fact, my greatest joy came from seeing them grow and advance their careers." Another dean argued, "It wasn't always about keeping competent department chairs or associate deans, but mentoring and advancing them into new leadership opportunities." Some fall deans sustained long-term energy and commitment by focusing on getting *their* faculty hires tenured. "Once my new crop of faculty is promoted and tenured, then I will consider my next move."

Deans in the fall of their career also shifted to give more time to serving their institutions. An *institutional* dean realized, "After four or five years when my college was on the right track, I spent almost three quarters of my time serving my institution. While I felt guilty not spending all my time on college affairs, chairing other dean searches and heading up presidential initiatives really renewed my interests and expanded my skill set. I felt valued by my institution, not just my college."

Tinker tactics also rekindled the academic soul of some deans. They looked inside and replanted the roots of their existence—learning. Few of the fall deans had returned to the fruits of writing and publishing, their original identity in the academy, but they discovered new areas of interest and excitement. "I hadn't planned on becoming an expert in finance, but the economic times required me to learn a new set of financial skills, and now my expertise is sought by other institutions." Other fall deans advanced their knowledge and reputation in strategic planning, donor development, athletic oversight, and leadership development.

Toehold Tactics: Explore Outside for New Ideas

Fall deans also practiced *toehold tactics* by searching outside the college or institution for new challenges at professional associations and national organizations and through interdisciplinary connections. Their newly acquired expertise and reputation was sought by other institutions and professional associations.

> My acquisition of a $23 million 'college-naming' donation quickly elevated me to the national speaking circuit on cultivating friends and funds. I just happened to be in the right place at the right time and picked up a few skills along the way. It has been quite a ride, but it is so far from the basic academic skills I honed to enter the academy and gain tenure.

Long-serving deans outlasted the average six-year tenure of deans and thus entered the stage of senior statesman for their state and national associations. They are called upon to head up state and national task forces, blue-ribbon committees, and their dean-alike associations:

When I entered the university as an assistant professor, being a dean wasn't even on my radar screen. To me, d-e-a-n was a four-letter word, the last job I would want. Flash forward, now, in my ninth year and as a senior dean, my colleagues elected me to serve as president of our dean association. Being dean is distant enough from my academic beginnings, but the thought of being "dean of deans" is daunting and humbling. But it required me to expand my vision, both horizontally across our institutions and vertically to state and national issues.

On the other hand, a dean of business observed, "Deans tend to have a myopic perspective; they talk only to other deans all the time." Just as faculty move from being specialists to generalists (Gardner, 1990; Gmelch & Miskin, 2004), some deans expanded from their college discipline to intercollegiate and national discourses. An example is a former corporate executive and now-transplanted engineering dean who brought together the deans of engineering, education, and technology to address national needs for science, math, and technology educators.

Mosaic Tactics: Zigzag Searching for New Challenges

Zigzag deans explored *mosaic tactics* in search of more fertile soil and greener pastures in alternative education-related professions, such as public school administration, state departments, or consulting. A dean who left his position to enter consulting reflected,

> I changed because of the confluence of two things. One, I was having less fun as dean after eight years, and I felt that I had made the impact that I would probably be capable of making, and if I had stayed for another four or five years, the degree of impact would diminish year to year. The other realization [was], if I waited any longer, I would lose the opportunity to make major changes, to have a major impact in my profession.

Another zigzag career dean entered higher education from the K–12 schools, served as dean for a number of years, and then became an executive search consultant:

> I served education as a classroom teacher, school administrator, district central office staff, assistant state superintendent of public instruction, administrator of my state administrator association, and, finally, dean of a private university. I knew the education system from top to bottom and

what it took to run academic enterprises. While some may say I get bored easily or learn a job quickly, and then get bored, I "finally" became a head-hunter to help universities find the right executives.

Exploration Tactics: Climb a New Mountain

Finally, some deans used *exploration tactics.* When they reached the top of the mountain and realized the deanship was not enough, or they realized they had climbed the wrong mountain, they changed mountains. Deans searched inside, outside, across, and beyond their current position and institution to avoid reaching a plateau and to keep their fire alive. One dean reflected,

> Being a dean wasn't enough and I wanted to do more than administer, something having greater impact on my profession. As dean, I had a big impact locally but a small influence nationally, and my notion was that as I grew and interacted with these people, I could make a difference in the lives of more people and more institutions. So, I left the deanship and I learned a new profession along the way.

Another dean in the fall season reflected, "After a dozen years at the helm of my college, what would be my legacy? Surely I could go beyond deaning." A dean in exploration realized, "The decline of my impact and fun in one area, and the mounting interest and excitement in another, both served as levers and pointed me in a new direction. . . . It was time to make a change." And this dean stopped his journey in the fall season and began ascending another mountain.

Seasoned Fall Deans' Advice to New Deans

Fall deans in our study willingly offered words of advice for new deans. Short of espousing another "pathological to-do list" or a David Letterman "Top Ten Cautions for Doomed Deans," here are eight reflective founts of wisdom from deans in the fall season of their deanship.

1. *Be clear why you want to be a dean.* Start at the end. Although some say leaving a legacy is overrated, ask yourself the following question: When I leave the deanship, what will others say about my tenure? Soon you will realize it is not "about you" but serving others. Read

the literature on servant leadership. And if you don't love your faculty, you can't lead. The real legacy you leave is in your people.

2. *Develop your leadership team.* Follow the sage advice of an African proverb: "If you want to travel fast, travel alone; if you want to travel far, travel together." As one fall dean put it, success is not about me, but we.

3. *Be a multiplier.* Use your intelligence to amplify the capabilities of people all around you, your staff, faculty, and leadership team. What's the best day in the life of a dean? When faculty get promoted! The worst day? When they are denied. How many of your faculty get promoted? How many programs are better today than the day you arrived? How many of your chairs became deans who make a difference? Multipliers attract and optimize their talents, create conditions for their creativity to be expressed, extend challenges, and instill ownership and accountability (Wiseman, 2010). As Harry Truman said, "You can accomplish anything in life, provided you don't mind who gets the credit" (McCullough, 1992, p. 564).

4. *Enhance leadership through learning.* What new books and journals are you now reading to advance your leadership thinking? Have you attended any seminars, workshops, or lectures to broaden your horizons? If it takes 10,000 hours to become an expert (Gladwell, 2008), how will you begin, develop, and sustain your deanship?

5. *Manage the political frame of your leadership.* The most common failure of executives is not working well with their superiors. Learn to educate and manage your provost. And develop a university-wide perspective with your dean colleagues and build a multilayered support network. Ultimately, you have to play well with others.

6. *Create a series of small wins.* Societal change does not occur overnight. Rosa Parks didn't just get on a bus one day and create the Civil Rights Movement. You can't expect your college to transform in your first year as dean. You must create and celebrate small wins (Weick, 1984) that move you toward your desired end.

7. *Find balance between your professional and personal lives.* Who are the deans with the most stress? Those who also care for children at home. You can't replay the ball game or ballet you missed. So find the right time in your career to be a dean. What is the toll your deanship will take on your spouse, partner, family? Can you balance the tradeoffs

in your lives? And, personally, can you take care of yourself—physically, socially, and intellectually?

8. *Love it or leave it.* The first year is too soon to make any rash judgments, but continually assess whether this is the right job for you. Are you having fun? Are you doing what satisfies you? Life is too short to do it for the perks—if there are any!

See chapter 6 for more advice to help beginning deans succeed.

Entering the Winter Season

Few of the fall deans we interviewed had preconceived career paths, as most entered the deanship serendipitously and often first served as "accidental" interim deans. One third of the deans in the fall season viewed the deanship as their capstone experience, whereas the other two thirds aspired to be a provost or president. This led us to the final season, the winter of a dean's life and the requisite question: Is there life after deaning?

The next chapter shares the voices of deans in the final season.

References

Arthur, M. B., & Fousseau, D. M. (1996). *The boundaryless career.* Oxford, England: Oxford University Press.

Buller, J. L. (2007). *The essential academic dean: A practical guide to college leadership.* San Francisco: Jossey-Bass.

Gardner, J. W. (1990). *On leadership.* New York: Free Press.

Gladwell, M. (2008). *Outliers: The story of success.* New York: Little, Brown, and Company.

Gmelch, W. H. (2003, January). *Seasons of a dean's life: Passages of the profession—keeping the fire alive.* American Association of Colleges for Teacher Education, New Orleans, LA.

Gmelch, W. H., Damico, S., Hopkins, D., & Mitchell, J. N. (2009). Passages in the profession: The academic deanship. *International Leadership Journal, 1*(3–4), 84–103.

Gmelch, W. H., & Miskin, V. D. (2004). *Chairing an academic department,* 2nd ed. Madison, WI: Atwood Publishing.

Gmelch, W. H., & Miskin, V. D. (2011). *Department chair leadership skills,* 2nd ed. Madison, WI: Atwood Publishing.

Hargreaves, A., & Fink, D. (2006). *Sustainable leadership*. San Francisco: John Wiley & Sons.

Hollander, D. (1991). *The doom loop system*. New York: Viking.

Kouzes, J. M., & Posner, B. Z. (2006). *A leader's legacy*. San Francisco: Jossey-Bass.

McCullough, D. (1992). *Truman*. New York: Simon & Schuster.

Weick, K. (1984). Small wins: Redefining the scale of social problems. *American Psychologist, 39,* 40–49.

Wiseman, L. (2010). *Multipliers*. New York: HarperCollins.

Wolverton, M., & Gmelch, W. H. (2002). *The college dean: Leading from within*. Westwood, CT: Oryx Press.

5

WINTER OF A DEAN'S CAREER

The Ending of an Era: Reflections on the Deanship

Although many of the deans interviewed for this study chose to leave the deanship, their reasons for leaving varied. Some sought promotion to a higher administrative role, such as provost or president; others moved to a new deanship at a different college or university; several were tempted by administrative positions in the private sector; still others found they were unhappy in administration and returned to the faculty; and some felt their career had run its course so they retired. In this chapter about the winter or ending of the deanship, we want to focus on those who leave for retirement or because they feel they have reached the end of their career as deans. During this time of transition, it is important that the winter dean anticipated what would follow. For many, the pace of life slows considerably. Even anticipating retirement or the end of administrative duties is a good time for reflection, a time to sit by the fire and chat with old friends—especially those who have already taken the next step on their way to what's next after deaning (Parks Daloz, Keen, Keen, & Daloz Parks, 1996). Do good memories remain and bad ones go away? Do individuals who have spent time in the deanship take the time to savor their successes? Or do they brood over the disappointments? The former deans we interviewed expressed highs from helping good faculty succeed, advancing their institutions, championing diversity and gender equity, and nurturing students. They also reflected on their lows, including lack of support from administration, poor communication with administration, faculty and staff who didn't join the vision, wasted resources because of human shortcomings, and conflicts with faculty and students.

Divergent Voices

The former deans interviewed were reflective about their experiences as leaders. Some felt they had been successful and others lamented lost opportunities. As they neared retirement, several dreamed of balance and serenity, if not in their profession, at least in their personal lives. For many, work had become their entire life. One of the prices they paid when they accepted the deanship was an incredible time commitment and the pressure to find balance in their lives. Their role as dean brought with it an identity. They had become "the Dean," and that self-concept often dictated who they socialized with, where they lived, how long they retained their position, and what lifestyle they led. Obviously, being in a leadership capacity through the years was an important part of their lives and provided them with pleasures as well as pressures. Being included in private receptions for well-known visitors to campus, entertaining major donors at football games and other sporting events in the box seats, having a voice in the strategic goals of the university, and receiving invitations to presidential balls, cocktail receptions, first-night performances, and so on are some of the perks that deans cited. Interestingly, the perks for many were enjoyed more fully earlier in their deanship. As they neared retirement, the "perks" often became irritating and unwelcome obligations. "Attending the President's Christmas party was alluring the first year I was in the deanship. By the 10th year, I dreaded it and left as soon as I felt I could without raising eyebrows. I had no desire to hobnob with upper administration and major funders when I had three wonderful grandchildren waiting for me at home."

Pressures during their tenure as dean transformed them from once unquestioning deans into individuals struggling to find balance between total academic immersion and a fulfilled private life. They often heard two divergent and competing voices in many phases of their deanship. Former deans reflected on those voices, and how, now that they had spent time in the role, they would guide others to listen as they entered and progressed through a deanship:

Be a **professional**, but also have a **personal** life.
Be a **leader**, but also a **scholar**.
Attend to **internal** demands, but also your **external** constituents.
Be a **cheerleader** for your colleagues, but also **evaluate** their performance.

The deans' ability to listen to both voices and develop a balanced life and work style depended on how well they made these tradeoffs. Did they believe their private life was as important as their professional? Had they found a way to balance the two? What price did deans pay for their venture into leadership? Where did it lead after their tenure as dean? What were the benefits? What were the costs? What was the impact of the deanship on personal life? At the end of the deanship was it worth it?

The effectiveness of deans seems to depend on their ability to juggle, balancing the tradeoffs between professional-personal, external-internal, scholar-leader, and cheerleader-evaluator, and the demands those roles place on their time and attention. A *tradeoff* is defined as an exchange of one interest for another, especially a giving up of something desirable (Greiff & Munter, 1980). Our interviews with winter deans nearing or at the end of their career provided insight into the tradeoffs they had made during the seasons of their deanships.

Attempting Balance: Professional and Personal Voices

The relationship between professorial and personal time resembles a "zero-sum" game for deans. All days have 24 hours, and most deans experience excessive stress from trying to balance their personal and professional lives. There are unavoidable tradeoffs as deans listen and try to juggle their professional and personal voices, realizing that both are vying for the same resources—time and attention. Time pressures dominate the dean's position. Meetings, heavy workload, deadlines, after-work activities, social obligations, excessive demands, and insufficient time for scholarship top the list of job stresses.

Deans interviewed for this study commented that they never dreamed the position would take the amount of time that it did; this observation was particularly common from those who had been deans for four or fewer years. All deans, however, agreed that the workload was heavy, and the expected activities stretched from early morning till late into the evening. In fact, many noted that the job is really 24/7. Statements echoed repeatedly by those interviewed ran along the lines of "The job impinges on my weekends and nights" and "I feel like I have no control over my own time." Another commented, "When you are the dean, you are responsible. I'm here to serve the college."

Given the heavy workload that never seems to cease, it was not surprising that finding balance between one's professional role as dean and that of an individual with a private life was a constant challenge. Time and energy were the culprits here. Many of those interviewed admitted they had failed to find a role balance. Others indicated they had resorted to scheduling personal time on their calendars; if they didn't, they would never have a life outside the deanship.

The lack of control over time and the amount of additional activities associated with the position affected both males and females, but in slightly different ways. The male deans were more constrained in their comments about the ways in which the deanship impinged upon their personal life. They were, however, sensitive to the many ways their jobs affected their spouses and children. As a result, the focus of many of the male deans' comments revolved around the way in which their schedules upset family routines, including dinner and opportunities to interact with their children. This clearly related to the regular 7 p.m. to 8 p.m. arrival time at home or frequent evening and weekend absences for university functions.

Several of the male deans talked about the way their position affected their wives and partners. For instance, one male dean commented that his wife didn't feel comfortable always being attached to his role. As he said, "It isn't necessarily negative, but still it's an issue." His wife felt that she had to monitor her actions in social situations. Deans' wives also felt pressure to watch what they wear to university events and, more importantly, watch what they say. Interestingly, a number of the wives did not like to attend university functions and avoided the ones that they felt were optional. As one dean explained, "If it's really important she'll go, but she doesn't like to do a lot of *that* stuff." None of the male deans interpreted these behaviors or feelings as lack of support for them.

The female deans interviewed had a slightly different perspective on the professional-personal balance. While all shared some of the same issues and tensions in trying to combine a personal and professional life, some encountered unique situations based on their marital status. Female deans interviewed in this study were married, single, or single mothers. The spouses of married female deans responded in similar ways to the wives of the male deans. In addition, the men who were married to the female deans in this study frequently found themselves relegated to the role of "spouse," a role many of them were not used to occupying. Some found that assigned role "uncomfortable." In spite of this, most of the female deans reported that their spouses were "good sports" and handled their role well. One female dean reported that her husband had "learned to watch what he said in public." Another female dean reported that she and her husband had different last names, a situation that was made uncomfortable when event name tags were prepared for him with her last name rather than his. Another female dean, now retired, had a husband who was never an academic and felt awkward attending university events; their solution was for him to never attend anything.

Males whose wives were deans faced role reversal. If there were children at home, they often became the primary caregiver, picking up children after school and ferrying them to school and friendship events. Also, these husbands in many cases became the partner who went to the grocery store, did the bulk of the cooking and cleaning, and ran most of the errands essential to maintaining a household. Some of the women deans felt uncomfortable with this shift in home responsibilities, but none reported this being an issue in their relationship with their husband.

Women deans who were single also experienced tension between their professional and personal lives. Professionally, they lived with most of the same time pressures faced by all deans but reported that, because of their marital status, faculty frequently didn't believe they had a life outside the deanship, nor that they might want one. Several of these women reported faculty intruding on their evenings and weekends and expecting them to always be available for even the smallest task. One reported that she finally bought a second home just so she could have an excuse to get out of town during weekends.

Those who appeared to have the most complex personal lives were the deans who were single mothers. Deans put in long and sometimes unpredictable hours. They also are required to travel—often. The women deans struggled with setting aside enough quality time to be with their children while successfully performing the role of dean. Finding and keeping quality day care or after-school care was a major concern; there was no spouse to pick up the slack. One female dean reported that she was expected to attend all home football games and participate in entertaining alumni. She commented, "I'm not a sports fan, and yet I have to go to football games as the dean. It has been difficult . . . particularly for my youngest son, who is still at home."

So through the years, how did deans obtain a balance between their professional and personal lives, or did they? One dean remembered that he and his wife went out to dinner every Friday evening because that was the one night of the week that he came home at a reasonable time. Others actually scheduled time on their calendars and learned over the years to take these schedules seriously. All admitted that it was difficult and that anyone entering the deanship should understand the type of responsibility and time commitment it entailed.

Balancing Scholarship and Leadership: From Fragmentation to Flow

The winter deans interviewed were reflective as they talked about their attempts to retain their identity as scholars while serving as leaders. Many deans struggled to find the right balance between being a scholar and a leader. They strove to retain their academic identity, and many still referred to themselves as scholars, but others saw them as only "deans." Ironically, one dean lamented, "Even when I published a book with a faculty colleague, the book cover introduced her with a long paragraph on her academic achievement and me as 'dean'—so much for my decades of research and scholarly identity!"

Several of the deans said that they believed, throughout their deanship, that they would return to the faculty (27%), and therefore felt it was wise to protect their scholarly interests (Wolverton & Gmelch, 2002). "I didn't want just one new line on my vita—*Dean*—to represent five long years I had spent in the academy as an administrator. Keeping up with my scholarship and being recognized for it is a part of my identity I don't want to lose." Nevertheless, almost all of the deans expressed frustration at their inability to spend much time pursuing academic agendas. "Having insufficient time to remain current in my discipline was one of the greatest stresses of my deanship" (Gmelch & Sarros, 1996). Most deans had the desire to stay current in their field and would have spent more time on their own academic endeavors if they could have, but found it virtually impossible because of leadership demands.

Again, the inner voices of the deans—one encouraging them to serve as leaders, another at the same time pushing them to satisfy their scholarly interests—were dissonant, competing, and contradictory. Serving as dean created a *fragmentation* of time and attention, whereas scholarship required the *flow* of optimal academic concentration. The competing forces of fragmentation and flow caused the deans dissonance in trying to balance their scholar and leader roles.

Deans' leadership work can be characterized as an unrelenting pace segmented by brevity, variety, and fragmentation (see Mintzberg's, 1973, and Jackson's, 2000, research on executives and deans, respectively). Their characterization of executive time represents the antithesis of quality time needed for scholarship. Yet the deans found it "really hard, really hard, to keep up with scholarship." Scholar-deans talked about the need for *flow*, not *fragmentation*. As expressed by Csikszentmihaly (1990), flow is an optimal experience requiring clear focus, a set of goals and responses, a sense of control over time, and immediate feedback—all with few distractions. This was not the leadership life of deans.

The deans testified that "time pressures" got to them. "You have no control over your own time in the deanship." Although some deans found ways to adjust to this, others "longed for quiet nights and long weekends." Another dean bemoaned that he "never left the office on a normal day before 7 p.m." Deans also lacked flow because of their lack of closure. The optimal experience vanished. As one dean succinctly put it, "I don't feel productive. I'm putting in longer hours and working harder all the time, and yet I'm finding it more and more difficult to see the results."

Winter deans reflected that over the seasons of their deanship they had experienced limited, if any, periods of concentrated time. One dean commented, "Numerous issues arrive on your desk all at once. You have to be good at multitasking." Many of the experienced winter deans tried to coach and mentor faculty with leadership potential for dean positions. They expressed their frustration, however, with trying to prepare future leaders only to hear that "some faculty watch what the deans are doing and decide they don't want to do it." Too often through the years the winter deans heard, "I don't know how you keep all the balls in the air at the same time." Even department chairs stated that they had no interest in a deanship because they enjoyed research more, liked teaching better, and disliked administration (McCarty & Reyes, 1987).

In retrospect, one winter dean reflected, "If I were to do anything differently, I would have tried to devote more time to my scholarship. I mean, that's the piece I feel most distant from right now." This frustration even came with a feeling of guilt: "What I feel bad about is my own scholarship.

I feel like I just left it withering in the lab." Some deans felt that without scholarship, they were not as effective as a leader for their faculty. "It is important to establish yourself as a strong academic and you have to have experienced high achievement in your field. . . . It gives you a sense of understanding of the research process and an important credibility with the faculty." In the end, however, deans found it almost impossible to balance their scholarship and leadership identities.

How did they protect their scholarship while serving as an academic leader? The winter deans who maintained some scholarship throughout their deanship did so by (a) entering the position with a research agenda already intact; (b) building a research team with faculty and graduate students and blocking time for them to meet and confer; (c) negotiating with the provost how scholarship would be rewarded and asking for moral—and graduate assistant—support; (d) selecting a dimension of their deanship to tie into their scholarship such as developing expertise in strategic planning, leadership, finance, teacher education, or other related decanal duties; (e) relying on staff and associate deans to take care of routine managerial tasks of the college; (f) finding an alternative office or laboratory to conduct research, write, and plan for teaching; (g) spending time in the flow zone (creative surroundings) and using these "flow" times each day for reflection and creativity; and (h) taking time for conferences in their disciplines, and not just the professional meetings requiring their presence as deans. In other words, the deans who were successful in keeping active in scholarship tried to build some flow into their fragmented academic life.

Balancing the Internal-External Voices: Managing the Relationships Molecule

Several former deans interviewed lamented they were not always able to control their internal-external tradeoff. Presidents, provosts, and faculty dictated some rules that became immutable conditions for deans' lives. Deans need to learn how to manage their "relationships molecule" (adapted from Onchen & Wass, 1974). Rather than envisioning their roles as managing inward to their college and staff, many retired deans likened their dean role as being in the center of the management molecule with the provost and president above, the college faculty and staff below, the campus deans and other university administrators on one side, and the external constituents on the other (Figure 5.1).

FIGURE 5.1
Dean's Relationships Molecule

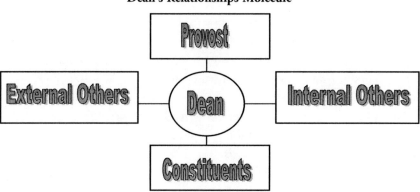

They reflected that finding themselves in this centered position in a management molecule was different from their previous faculty and department chair roles. This molecule model shows the added dimensions the deans took on when they left their previous roles to become deans. Previously, managing the provost, building collaborative leadership within the college, managing relationships with campus colleagues, and establishing networks with stakeholders were not within their purview. Winter deans pointed out that they could not always control the pressures for their time and attention from within the university and among the outside constituents. They perceived themselves as role prisoners caught between external challenges of building collaborative relationships and internal demands of managing and leading the university. As one dean observed about her relationships, "Being a dean is a challenge from different directions every day, whether it's faculty, whether it's curriculum, whether it's legislators, donors—it's like one big chess game played on multidimensional layers. That's what makes it fun."

Deans interviewed for this study at or nearing the end of their deanship agreed that their main responsibilities throughout the years involved the highest level of communication and interpersonal skills in dealing with internal and external constituents. In fact, the lion's share of a dean's life appeared to be spent establishing personal relationships with others in order to move the college's agenda forward. Deans found this work important, challenging, and sometimes intense. Several deans observed that good interpersonal skills were essential to be a successful dean. As one winter dean commented, "The most important skill for any dean is the ability to work with multiple constituencies of people. It's those people skills that I think are the most important."

The provost was the key upward relationship for the deans we interviewed. Because they reported to provosts and provosts controlled resources, winter deans reflected that they were acutely aware of the importance of this relationship. They made the effort to keep the provost fully informed and educated about educational issues. A typical comment was, "Anything that has impact, I made sure the provost knew."

Sometimes the deans felt their communication with the provost was open, respected, and reciprocated. Other times they felt the provost glazed over and didn't hear what they were saying. Regardless, the deans felt that the relationship was critical for the college, its programs and its image. One dean commented, "The one time that was the worst for me was when a new provost came on board who really did not understand education." Another dean vented,

> One of the dissatisfying things was having to keep educating the *damn* provost about what to do. I mean I had this constant battle to keep central administration educated about what it is I did and why it was important, and, in fact, central administration should be a dean's biggest supporter. But often I found myself spending an inordinate amount of time educating them as to why they should support us, and when they finally came around, then we were almost out of gas.

If the relationship between the provost and dean is termed an upward relationship, then a downward relationship involves the dean and the faculty and staff within the college. Deans reported that a major portion of their time was devoted to informal and formal meetings with associated deans, department chairs, faculty, and staff to work through changing curricular or program issues, respond to needs and directives, and solve other college problems. Most deans indicated that they worked hard to build relationships among college constituents, using terms such as "nurtured and developed faculty and students and staff," and "spent a lot of time walking up and down the halls and talking to the faculty." The feelings of most deans seemed to be captured by such comments as "Deans create a climate where people feel valued; where faculty, students, and staff feel this is a community and that we all have a vested interest in it." Winter deans especially realized the importance of faculty relationships, and shared comments like that of one dean who succincly stated, "If you don't have the faculty on your side, you can't do squat."

The third internal relationship deans have is with other campus deans and individuals outside the college who are influential within the university community, such as staff in various university offices and campus-wide committees. Often, deans felt compelled to work with other deans and influence leaders on campus to advance the work of their colleges. In these relationships, the dean was alternately engaged in informing them, negotiating with them, and marketing the college's interests. One dean summed up the bridge-building work as follows: "There was a real need to work collaboratively with others both up and down the chain of command, and I had a lot of public relations responsibilities."

Several deans spoke particularly about their relationships with deans of other colleges on campus, some because of natural collaboration, shared authority, and responsibility for interdependent programs. For example, education deans relied on arts and sciences deans in teacher preparation as "it takes a campus to educate a teacher." Engineering deans worked closely with science deans to deliver the "right mathematics classes required to prepare engineers." However, one dean also observed that relationships with other deans on his campus were difficult, stating, "College deans on this campus were all equally hard-pressed, so it was hard for us to work together. We were all overwhelmed and felt so alone. It was tough to feel collegial among the deans. . . . There was no one to help us get together."

The three internal audiences previously discussed have traditionally been the ones with whom deans interacted most. However, recently, there has been additional pressure on deans to devote more time to external relationships because of the increase in the number of external constituencies. Winter deans in our interviews mentioned their external board of governors, national professional organizations, legislators, alumni, donors and businesses, schools, and community members as external audiences with whom they had frequent contact. Several deans mentioned national and state reasons for increased contact with external constituents. One experienced dean still in the role commented, "We are going to have to respond to all the challenges to education at the state and national levels. These pressures have been increasing. I felt strongly that in education, we need to connect our work more closely to schools or community."

Often, building these external relationships takes a significant amount of time. As one dean said, "I spent a lot of time in the legislature educating them, and I spent a lot of time with donors. I spent a lot of time on the national scene and a lot of time trying to educate other deans to get them to appreciate the national education situation. I was spending maybe a third of my time doing the outside stuff." Yet deans, for the most part, seemed to feel that developing external relationships was worthwhile and were willing to give it their time and effort, "to be more involved and more visible, building more of a presence for their college in the state."

The demands on a dean's time to build and maintain relationships with various constituents were significant. As in the other areas of a dean's life, balancing the internal relationships with the external ones is essential. As portrayed in the Dean's Relationship Molecule, they need to continually vary their view, not just looking up and down, but also looking to their sides as they build relationships and communicate with critical constituents. All are important relationships, and deans cannot neglect any if they wish to be effective leaders.

After leaving the deanship, winter deans lamented that all of the hours and dedication they spent building their molecules and establishing trust relationships would "now go for naught!" "You spend so much of your time building your political and social capital to become an effective dean, but once you leave, the efforts are lost."

Cheerleader-Evaluator: Dealing With Psychological Tradeoffs

The deans we interviewed believed they should champion faculty and be cheerleaders for their accomplishments. However, as those in the winter of their deanship so aptly stated, they were also aware that, ultimately, they had the fiduciary responsibility to evaluate faculty. A national study reported that most deans perceived themselves to be "both faculty and administrator" (62%), 32% perceived themselves as primarily "administrators," and only a small portion (6%) viewed themselves solely as "faculty" (Wolverton & Gmelch, 2002). It appears that the more forcefully deans rowed toward the shores of administration, the more distant they became in their ability to identify with faculty. In effect, their evaluator role created an island of administration, psychologically isolated and distant from their faculty colleagues. A retired arts and sciences dean explained,

> Back when I was a member of the English faculty, every morning I would join my colleagues in the Union for coffee and a bagel. Most mornings, our discussion for the day centered on the latest foolish action of the dean. Then I became the dean, and I realized I could no longer join my colleagues nor share in their discussion. I had become who they were talking about!

All of the deans in this study struggled during their deanship to find the right balance. One of the most difficult roles they attempted to balance in academe was the one they played as cheerleader and evaluator. Like Janus, the two-faced god of Roman mythology, a dean is viewed at times as duplicitous, bragging expansively about faculty one moment and denying them promotion or tenure the next. One face the dean makes public is that of "college champion," cheering the college's merit in countless arenas. This face brags openly at Rotary meetings about faculty accomplishments and advances their success stories at the Chamber of Commerce. This face promotes faculty achievements in comments to prospective students and their parents, points out faculty capabilities to community college and school district partners, and continually informs campus administration of faculty value.

The other face a dean reveals is one that evaluates that same braggedabout faculty and sometimes finds them lacking. This face frowns with concern over insufficient scholarship although an individual is an exemplary teacher. This face makes the hard decision to deny promotion or continued employment even though the person is a terrific team player and is well loved by colleagues and administrators alike.

To be a cheerleader and an evaluator at the same time is never easy. The deans interviewed expressed their frustration in balancing the two. Several commented that they enjoyed the advocate role. One liked being the "chief advocate" for the school. Another talked about faculty being the "heart of the institution" and found deep satisfaction in allowing faculty to "grow and develop in terms of their own professional careers or interests while making sure that they remained connected to the mission of the school." Many saw "selling the college" as a primary responsibility—especially, interestingly enough, on campus. Convincing the provost of the value of the college appeared to be an ongoing goal. Obtaining visibility for the college on a national level also was seen as important, and several commented on their fundraising efforts designed to support faculty attendance at national conventions and professional meetings.

Several deans also stressed their efforts in promoting the faculty with community and alumni groups. The consensus was that, as deans, one had to go to a lot of university activities—even when going home was preferred—because their colleges had to be represented. For some, this meant learning how to schmooze. A few found it difficult, but essential as deans, to become "social butterflies." "It is not that I didn't like people. I love people, but I'm just not one that instantly goes up and starts chitchatting with somebody, and you have to do that. . . . Alumni expect you to do it," commented one dean. Overall, deans saw themselves as chief communicators for their colleges and primary cheerleaders of their colleges' programs and people.

Most of the winter deans interviewed were extremely vocal about their roles as evaluators. Several commented about the difficulty in making the hard calls in regard to tenure and promotion especially because they knew it was "affecting people's lives." Deans were aware that they were the ones who had to make the "difficult personnel calls," and they did not take this responsibility lightly. Many had agonized over their decisions. As one respondent commented, "I sought broad consultation. . . . So many of these cases are professional judgments." Another commented that he had received the "dart board" award from human resources as a result of removing a senior faculty member from a long-established role because he was killing the program. But in removing him, the dean had to find something face-saving for him to do that would "honor his longtime commitment to the institution." Another dean remarked, "I could do personnel stuff and do it well, but it was difficult. It was hard because you knew you were affecting people's lives." Several also talked of the balance in the tenure and promotion journey, in other words, trying to encourage a person as he or she grew professionally and yet having to later assess the person's development as insufficient for continued employment or promotion. One mentioned the dismissal of a tenured teacher. He commented that just tolerating her until retirement would have been the easiest solution but not the right solution. "I tried to counsel her, but she was very angry and . . . not at all satisfied."

Over and over again, the deans commented about the time they spent throughout their careers making evaluative decisions—especially those that concerned people. One dean said that in 20 years, he had had only one grievance, but that it "broke his heart" because it was based on the notion that he did not support an assistant professor. The dean felt he had provided tremendous support for the faculty member throughout the pretenure years. Unfortunately, his encouragement was not enough. The assistant professor did not have a record sufficient for tenure.

It is clear that the deans interviewed enjoyed being a cheerleader much more than being an evaluator. Given the choice, most would turn outward the face of promoter, advocate, encourager, and fan. However, deans also accepted that they were the face of evaluator, critic, assessor, and judge. Balancing the two—cheerleader and evaluator—was a continual struggle. Those deans who went back to faculty after their deanships "didn't miss the evaluator roles" they played. They were relieved not to have to make personnel "judgment" calls. However, one former dean cautioned, "Be careful what you do to people as you go up the ladder as someday you may come back down." Another dean stated, "Some colleagues harbored the ill will created when I was dean, and it made it difficult to return as a colleague."

In sum, former deans recalled feeling trapped in their self-expectations of performing dual and competing roles. The competing inner voices were commonplace and sometimes they heard dissonant songs. They recounted and advised that, without personal goals, ethics, and objectives to guide them in making tradeoff decisions, the demand of activities dominating one side of the scale could engulf the dean's time, energy, and credibility. Without balance, deans left their position in a state of frustration and imbalance. Where did they go?

Life After the Deanship

Is there life after deaning? Do most deans stay in the position until retirement? Do any go on to provost positions and presidencies? What percentage returns to teaching? Are there other opportunities and options open for those who have served in the deanship?

In one national study of deans, their most frequent choice was either to move up to a higher position in academic leadership (22%) or to move back to faculty ranks (27%). Another set of deans expressed no interest in moving (17%) and an equal number thought their next move would be retirement (17%). Only 15% had a desire to move to another dean's position at a similar institution (7%) or a more prestigious institution (8%). A few saw them-selves changing to a nonacademic leadership position (2%) (Wolverton & Gmelch, 2002).

In reality, the choices many deans made at the end of their deanship were markedly different from what they dreamed would be their next move. Others progressed, season after season, through the years exactly as they had visualized. We tracked a decade of our colleagues' career paths, interviewed dozens of former deans, and inquired into the adjustments they made during their transitions. Although the percentages in Figure 5.2 reported what deans envisioned, the reality of the career path of many was quite different yet personally enriching and challenging.

Most of the deans we interviewed did climb to a higher position, go on to another deanship, return to the faculty, or retire. There were several who took a less familiar route.

One dean at a prestigious private university left to take a provost's posi-tion, found the role tedious, and left to work in Washington, D.C., for a

FIGURE 5.2
The Dean's Next Move

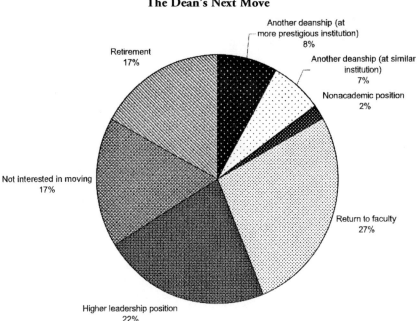

private educational consulting firm. She commented that she enjoyed "leaving the red tape of academe" behind.

Another education dean was given the opportunity to leave the academic side of the house and became a vice president for development at her institution. Having the people skills necessary, she enjoyed the position and was quite successful.

Still another individual who had held two previous and successful deanships discovered that he enjoyed working with older nontraditional students and accepted a presidency at an urban community college.

When the directorship of a national accrediting body became available, one dean left a successful deanship in the Midwest to take on the role. His experience as a dean has been cited numerous times as being an asset for the position he now holds.

Once they retired, several deans accepted one- to three-year appointments overseas assisting developing colleges and universities. Countries like the United Arab Emirates actively recruited these professionals to guide their higher education efforts.

Still other deans chose totally different lifestyles upon retirement and enjoyed quieter, less stressful days. And, sadly, a few of the deans we interviewed for the study passed away before they had the time to take pleasure in a life after deaning.

Ultimately, what happens when deans leave the position? Our former deans felt much less pressure and stress when they no longer were always "on point" for every responsibility. If they returned to faculty, their inner voices became less dissonant and conflicting. After all, they were faculty. But they also missed the action and excitement that administration had delivered to their desks. Personally, their families and spouses or partners were, for the most part, happier, because they had better working hours and more weekends free for the choosing. They found more discretionary time and liked being able to once again pick and choose their activities, whether university committees, community engagements, professional opportunities, or leisure fun. Those who returned to teaching raved about "found time" and improved family life. However, they also left the deanship with a profound desire to impart sage advice to fellow deans and those aspiring to be deans. We have included much of their "voice of experience" counsel in chapter 6.

References

Csikszentmihaly, M. (1990). *Flow: The psychology of optimal experience.* New York: HarperCollins.

Gmelch, W. H., & Sarros, J. (1996). How to work with your dean: Voices of American and Australian department chairs. *The Department Chair, 6*(4), 1–19.

Greiff, B. S., & Munter, P. K. (1980). *Tradeoffs: Executive, family and organizational life.* New York: New American Library.

Jackson, J. J. (2000). *Decanal work: Using role theory and the sociology of time to study the executive behavior of college of education deans.* Unpublished doctoral dissertation, Iowa State University, Ames.

McCarty, D. J., & Reyes, P. (1987). Organizational model of governance: Academic deans' decision-making styles. *Journal of Teacher Education, 38*(5), 2–8.

Mintzberg, H. (1973). *The nature of managerial work.* New York: Harper & Row.

Onchen, W., Jr., & Wass, D. L. (1974). Management time: Who's got the monkey? *Harvard Business Review, 52*(6), 75–80.

Parks Daloz, L. A., Keen, C. H., Keen, J. P., & Daloz Parks, S. (1996). *Common fire: Leading lives of commitment in a complex world.* Boston: Beacon Press.

Wolverton, M., & Gmelch, W. H. (2002). *The college dean: Leading from within.* Westwood, CT: Oryx Press.

6

DEAN DEVELOPMENT
Personal, Institutional, and Professional Implications

The deans participating in this study experienced socialization processes similar to those encountered by other executives in the corporate and private sectors. However, unlike the socialization of chief executive officers in the private sector, socialization of academic leaders appears to be left to chance. Institutions of higher learning must realize the impact socialization techniques can have on a dean's productivity and propensity toward longevity or departure from their institutions.

Because most academic leaders begin their training in academia as researchers and teachers, they rarely anticipate or experience the roles and responsibilities of the deanship. Therefore, throughout their academic career and until they find themselves in the role, they have had minimal management and leadership training. This supports the premise that one of the most glaring shortcomings in leadership as a study is the scarcity of sound research on the training and development of leaders (Conger & Benjamin, 1999).

As explored in chapter 1, the leadership development of deans is a process that extends over many years, through all of the seasons of their professional lives—spring, summer, winter, and fall. Our research suggests that there are three spheres essential to developing deans: (a) a *conceptual understanding* of the unique roles and responsibilities encompassed in academic leadership; (b) the *skills* necessary to achieve the results through working with faculty, staff, students, other administrators, and external constituencies; and (c) the practice of *reflection* to learn from past experiences and perfect the art of deaning. These three spheres, present throughout the seasons of a dean's life, vary in intensity. When and how a dean develops each of these is dependent upon his adaptability to act and react, the environment in which she practices, the experiences he encounters, and the support she receives from others.

In this final chapter, we first highlight some of the strategies deans used in the seasons of their lives and then conclude with suggestions and effective practices that those in or entering the deanship may use to foster their own leadership development.

Seasons of a Dean's Life: Personal Development Strategies

To assist our readers in identifying strategies that may foster dean leadership development, we have provided Table 6.1. In addition, we have grouped the strategies under the three components of leadership development discussed earlier (conceptual understanding, skill development, and reflective practice) and across three levels of interventions: personal, institutional, and professional. The policy implications and recommendations included were garnered from the dean interviews and the leadership intuition of the authors as practicing scholar-deans with over 50 years of collective experience gleaned at 10 universities.

At the *institutional level*, we define the scope of the job through systemic efforts and seamless approaches to the selection, socialization, and development of deans. Prior to and during the deanship, universities must provide for continual professional leadership development through such strategies as in-house retreats, personalized professional development plans, and periodic reviews and renewals (sabbaticals). At the *professional level*, organizations like the American Council on Education (ACE) and the American Association for Colleges of Teacher Education (AACTE) must provide forums, conferences, and literature to guide deans in dealing with strategic issues in the academy and deanship. Finally, at the *personal level*, deans need assessment, feedback, personal advice, and other means to grow in their jobs to become effective leaders. On a personal basis, deans need to engage in networking, seek mentors, look for coaching opportunities, and practice reflective writing.

Deans' Development of Conceptual Understanding: Habits of Mind

Cognitively, deans must explore and understand the many dimensions of leadership by using mental models, frameworks, and role theory. In other

TABLE 6.1
Strategies for Dean Leadership Development

Level of Intervention	Leadership Development Component		
	Conceptual Understanding *Habits of Mind*	Skill Development *Habits of Practice*	Reflective Practice *Habits of Heart*
Personal	Higher education classes Leadership conferences Books and journals Shift in mental models	External seminars (ACE) Assessment of skills and fit Support groups Short commercial seminars Executive MBA or MPA	Journaling Reflective practice Mentors, coaches, networks Values clarification Faith
Institutional	Orientation process Seamless socialization Executive development Administrative sabbatical Team indoctrination Professional stipend	Campus leadership seminars Internships and shadowing Mentorships College deans on campus Colleague deans off campus Professional development	Annual reviews Deans' council Provost 1-1 sessions Campus confidants Deans' therapy sessions Mentor programs
Professional	Generic IHE organizations New Deans Institute Dean associations Networks Quondam deans	Leadership literature Dean-a-like organizations Conference workshops Skill-based training Professional organizations	Internet networks Consortia Regional, state, national networks National cohort programs

Note: ACE, American Council on Education; *IHE,* Innovative Higher Education; *MBA,* master of business administration; *MPA,* master of public administration.

words, deans must form new *habits of mind* as they move from specialist (i.e., a faculty member with an individual research agenda) to generalist (i.e., an administrator with responsibility to support numerous research agendas, including those germane to the college as a whole, as an academic leader). Deans must also understand how universities operate and recognize the unique organizational, political, and social characteristics of institutions of higher education.

Two commonalities surfaced from our interviews: (a) As deans moved into leadership positions, their concept of the job shifted; and (b) although some similarities existed across all types of organizations, deans in institutions of higher education faced challenges that were not typical of managers and leaders in other organizations. As academicians move into the deanship from previous positions in the academy, they start to perceive themselves differently. For example, using Bolman and Deal's (2008) terms, and the researchers from Iowa State University, department chairs predominantly think in terms of their human and structural frames of leadership. Most of their time revolves around faculty, staff, and students. They focus on curriculum, course offerings, and the calendar. As chairs and other individuals we studied moved into the deanship, however, they became more aware of two additional frames that also demanded their attention, the political and symbolic. Now as administrators, the importance of having good relationships beyond college and university became apparent. Spending time in the state capital became essential and selling the college and its programs to alumni, friends, politicians, and the press occupied their time in ever-increasing amounts. The deans soon recognized their role: chief cheerleader for the college (Gmelch, Reason, Schuh, & Shelley, 2002).

Personal Level

Although there is little organized training for deans, they can expand their conceptual understanding of the position by attending classes on higher education leadership topics, such as budgeting, strategic planning, curriculum development, and current issues. *The Chronicle of Higher Education* and other higher education trade magazines and academic journals also provide deans with critical background and perspectives on higher education issues. Many of the deans we interviewed attended general higher education conferences, such as the ACE, the AACTE, the American Association of Colleges and Universities, and professional dean associations in business, pharmacy, and arts and sciences, to name a few. These and other associations feature workshops, presentations, and symposia on higher education administration. Several deans commented that these conferences provided them with an environmental scan of higher education as they moved from disciplinary specialist to a university generalist. These and other professional development efforts can aid deans in gaining a better grasp on how others go about balancing management with leadership, scholarship with leadership, and their personal lives with professional obligations.

Institutional Level

It became apparent throughout our study that universities and colleges need to design and deliver programs to address the seamless selection, socialization, and development of deans. Some institutions with unique missions, such as land-grant universities and faith-based institutions, have developed systematic leadership team meetings designed to understand and advance their unique market position and core beliefs. For example, one dean mentioned a systematic leadership development program on campus that brought in higher education scholars to provide them with an understanding of how universities work. Another faith-based institution had monthly readings and discussions with the president, vice president, and deans on what it meant to be a Jesuit university.

None of the deans reported having any type of beneficial formal orientation to the university as a new dean. One dean did report that he was sent to "university orientation" for his training. He learned that there were 48 bells in the university campanile. Many of the deans interviewed felt that an orientation session would have provided them with a more seamless socialization into the institution. Even those who had been at the institution for a number of years in other roles felt that such a process would incorporate training across all phases of dean acclimation. Prior to conferring the deanship, universities need to systematically invest in and formally train the future leaders of their institutions. They need to think about "growing" their own deans, cultivating promising academic leaders, and spotting them early on in their academic careers, as many corporations have done. These organizations have ensured that their companies are "built to last" over the years by developing their own executives from within the organization (Collins & Porras, 1994). Throughout all seasons of the dean's career, universities must (a) provide for continued professional leadership development through in-house retreats; (b) allocate professional development stipends dedicated to allowing deans to take advantage of workshops, seminars, books, and journals; and (c) assist with professional leaves after a designated number of years of service as an academic administrator, especially if the administrator is phasing out of the leadership role and reentering the faculty ranks.

Professional Level

Once again, the deans interviewed mentioned general higher education organizations, such as the AACTE and ACE, as important components in developing their conceptual understanding of higher education and how universities work. In addition, disciplinary-specific seminars, such as the weeklong New Deans' Institute sponsored by the AACTE, helped orient newly appointed deans into their positions. Other professional organizations also provided specific conferences and institutes to socialize deans into their leadership positions and facilitate networking among deans.

When deans became more senior in their tenure or moved out of their roles, they spoke of training future generations of deans by mentoring, counseling, and teaching those new to the endeavor. A few retired or former deans who have experienced all of the seasons of a deanship and been through the rite of passage referred to themselves as "quondam" deans, willing to serve as key resources for the socialization and success of the next generation of deans. In some instances, former deans found their stage of "life after the deanship" was to serve as interim deans while institutions searched for new leadership. Other former deans served hazardous duty cleaning up a college or school before a new dean arrived.

Deans' Skill Development: Habits of Practice

It is not uncommon to hear someone say, "That person is a natural leader." The observation is usually made about an individual who seems to know intuitively the right approach to every situation. In reality, born leaders are few. Most, including those who have accepted deanships, need instruction, experience, nurturing, and time to develop the skills they need. They develop through *habits of practice*. The dilemma for deans as leaders arises because the necessary components of skill development are seldom, or insufficiently, available. Deans quickly realize that the expertise and behaviors they need to be successful leaders will be acquired for the most part piecemeal while they are on the job. Also, the skills department chairs and associate deans acquire in their ascension to the deanship are not always adequate or appropriate for deans. It seems ironic that the individuals our colleges and universities rely upon most for leadership are essentially self-taught. Their skills develop gradually and often haphazardly, the result of arbitrary training, inadequate feedback, and random mentoring.

Personal Level

A personal development plan starts with an assessment of the match between the types of skills deans bring to their positions and the demands of the job as well as the job fit with the institution. Deans unfamiliar with managerial subtleties need to seek out opportunities to hone their executive skills. The majority, however, develop their leadership skills on their own with little or no formalized training or assistance. Many rely upon management literature and pore over books and articles offering administrative models and management strategies. Even then, the tasks that veteran deans have learned to manage can stymie inexperienced leaders. Lacking knowledge and skill, many rely on trial-and-error problem solving, an approach that can frustrate faculty who want decisive leaders with ready solutions.

The professional development market is replete with commercial venues for management seminars, from performance evaluation to principled negotiations. These individual programs tend to be relatively short, from half-day seminars to a few days in length, but with little or no follow-up. Not so abundant are skill development programs tailor-made for academic leaders. A dean with the resources of time and money (i.e., a professional development stipend) can find a myriad of opportunities for executive development. Unfortunately, these opportunities may still be lacking in the specific skills training essential for leaders in academe.

Institutional Level

Institutions can encourage professional development through their offices of human resource development. A few institutions provide in-house workshops and seminars that focus on real-life leadership and campus issues. However, few institutions tailor-make their programs for executive development. Most programs are designed for midmanagement and address more managerial issues, personnel practices, legal issues, and budget development, not the difficult leadership and ethical dilemmas often plaguing deans. One dean had been part of a yearlong professional development program designed to stimulate and sustain skill development through practice and reinforcement of key executive skills. Other institutions have provided executive internships and exchanges across colleges and campuses for up-and-coming university administrators. Sitting deans typically can't take advantage of these opportunities because they are continually in the line of fire and occupied with daily duties.

In-house mentorships are also a source of skill development for deans. One dean advised that a new dean should get a mentor—someone who can listen and help with decisions. Unfortunately, the more experienced deans who could mentor these novice leaders are not readily available or are seen as a risk. Developing deans may shy away from asking their more experienced colleagues for help. They worry that their lack of knowledge will be perceived as a weakness. However, the pairing of seasoned and new deans in a safe environment provided some of the deans in our study with a "critical friend" to consult with as confidants. Internships, shadowing experiences, and exchanges developed by universities to facilitate skill acquisition also provide a venue for dean development.

Professional Level

Skill development training opportunities are minimal; few provide systematic preparation or follow-up. If funding and time allow, some deans attend workshops or institutes offered by professional education organizations like AACTE and ACE, others go to specific managerial training like that offered by Harvard or Bryn Mawr, and still others attend conferences focused on some aspect of administration like those presented by the Council for Advancement and Support of Education. Across colleges and schools of education, deans from similar institutions have also formed separate organizations (research university deans, comprehensive university deans, and liberal arts deans and directors) to further their discussions and address common problems. Organizations such as the Council for Colleges of Arts and Sciences and the American Assembly of Collegiate Schools of Business also provide conferences and institutes to socialize their deans into their leadership positions.

Overall, deans who maintain active membership in broad-based higher education professional organizations reap the benefit of learning more generalized approaches to academic leadership than they once received from their specialized, discipline-centered professional organizations (Wolverton & Gmelch, 2002). The deans we interviewed didn't believe there was much in the literature to read about being a dean. Although many of those interviewed expressed concern about keeping up with the literature in their own discipline, most recognized that leadership had become the discipline within which they must hone their skills. From the general higher education associations' annual meetings, publications, and networks, deans learn the language, literature, and innovations of higher education (Green & McDade, 1994).

Deans' Development Through Reflective Practice: Habits of Heart

Understanding the role of dean and possessing the requisite skills to be one were not sufficient for deans to believe they could become successful. Leadership development for many of the deans we interviewed was an inner journey, and often the most difficult part of their professional growth. Self-knowledge, personal awareness, and corrective feedback are all part of a leader's development. Moral, ethical, and spiritual dimensions were necessary for many to complete their leadership journey and feel grounded in their *habits of heart.* When a group of Australian deans was asked what skill they needed the most to be an effective dean, one who oversaw engineering responded, "Know thyself—I have to know myself before I can lead my team and faculty."

Leadership development is very much about finding one's voice (Kouzes & Posner, 1987). Because credibility and authenticity lie at the heart of good leadership, many of the deans we interviewed felt that determining and identifying their guiding beliefs and assumptions were at the heart of becoming good deans. This substantiates the critical need for structured feedback, reflection, and self-awareness as reflective strategies if deans are to flourish.

As reflected in Table 6.1, institutions, professions, and deans themselves must build in time and mechanisms to become reflective practitioners.

Personal Level

Although managers reflect-in-action, seldom do they reflect on their reflection-in-action (Schon, 1983). Hence, this crucially important dimension of dean development tends to remain private and inaccessible to others. The deans we talked to felt alone; they felt that others did not understand them and that they did not have access to dialogue with job-alike colleagues. They tended to remain private and inaccessible to others. Moreover, because awareness of one's intuitive thinking usually grows out of practice in articulating it to others, deans often have little access to their own reflection-in-action. Perhaps the most reflective activity in which deans engaged was through journal writing, personal dictation, or other means of reflecting and imprinting their professional experience. A new, "springtime" dean made three entries into his journal every evening: "What went well today, what got in the way, and what I would do differently tomorrow." After three years and 1,500 pages entered into his journal, his reflective intuition led the way into the summertime of his deanship.

Deans believed reflection helped them prioritize and weigh their professional careers against their personal lives. Faith and value clarification also provided some deans with an inner sense of commitment and fulfillment.

The inner core values helped deans face new challenges every day and gave them a fresh new spirit.

Institutional Level

Leadership development does not take place within a vacuum. It is nourished and flourishes best within a group or with trusted colleagues acting as mentors, partners, and coaches. Institutions have formal structures in place, such as the deans' council, academic partnerships, and annual reviews to provide deans with systematic means of formative evaluation and feedback. Many deans also have developed informal deans' groups that meet without the provost over coffee or a meal in a "safe" environment, so they may reflect and explore common issues and needs. For many, these become "therapy" sessions. One-on-one meetings with the provost also provide a venue for discussion of a variety of topics from campus issues to "the meaning of life." For some, having a confidant outside the college provided a supportive bonding experience to explore ethical and moral dilemmas.

Professional Level

Professional organizations helped our deans establish networks. Through attending national conferences and professional development programs, they connected with their colleagues, formed personal relationships, and developed networks of confidants. Like the freshman experience in college, springtime deans attending the New Deans' Institute formed bonds with other new deans that lasted throughout their tenure as dean and beyond. They met at annual meetings and kept in touch via phone and e-mail throughout the year. By helping deans across institutions, states, and countries consider what it is they really do, how they do it, why they do it, and what difference they make, professional organizations go a long way toward creating and supporting a cadre of effective campus leaders.

Advice for New Deans

As we interviewed deans, practicing and retired, advice for those who were just beginning flowed freely. All of the deans were ready to counsel, guide, instruct, and warn those who were entering the ranks. They urged beginning deans to keep the vision alive, advance the college, hire well, attract and maintain good faculty, continue to lead, give back to the profession, and have fun! The deans in our study didn't have to be prompted; they willingly espoused words of advice for new deans. Possibly motivated by their need for generativity or just generosity, here is some of the sage advice they shared:

> *Pay attention to national issues in education.* It is up to you to keep the president and provost apprised of issues impacting education. That means you had better do your homework. Read *The Chronicle of Higher Education*—the articles, not the position descriptions. Subscribe to *Education Week, Inside Higher Education, University Business,* and other publications that can be skimmed quickly and check daily for news sound bites.
>
> *Become friends with state Department of Education staff and state and national legislators.* You will need these individuals in your corner if you expect to forward initiatives or make change.
>
> *Develop a university-wide perspective.* Be aware of the other colleges' goals, their niche programs, and future dreams. And make sure they know about yours. Collaborate every chance you get.
>
> *Identify a mentor.* Find someone you admire who is willing to have lunch with you every couple of weeks, someone you can bounce ideas off of and share concerns. Sometimes the best person for this important job is someone who is not a part of your campus.
>
> *Recognize that there is a difference between friends and colleagues.* One of the most difficult aspects of being a dean is realizing that you cannot socialize as freely as you once did with faculty. Everyone takes notice of who goes to lunch with the dean, so spread yourself around.
>
> *Remember that knowledge is power.* Everyone likes to think they have the inside track on the latest happenings in the college, so be careful what you share because even if you think it will remain confidential it seldom does.
>
> *Take time for professional development.* Too often, beginning deans feel that they should support every faculty member's opportunity for professional development and ignore their own. Don't hesitate to take advantage of workshops on fundraising, leadership training, dean conferences, and so on.
>
> *Establish a strong academic record.* Carve out time for your scholarship. Have your administrative assistant block your time one morning a week or stay out of the office every Friday morning to stay current in

your personal research—even if it shifts to leadership or a related emphasis.

Take care of yourself—physically, socially, and intellectually. Give yourself permission to leave early on Tuesdays and Thursdays to work out at the gym. Take time to go have a manicure or visit the beauty shop. If you are busy with college-related events all weekend, take time during the week to drop off the dry cleaning, do the shopping, or clean the garage.

Take the "rubber chicken test." Take this right away—even before you accept a deanship. The test is simple. Ask yourself if you enjoy eating chicken dinners with strangers two to three times a week. If the answer is no, you need to reconsider your decision. Deans spend an inordinate number of nights at banquets, scholarship events, alumni gatherings, and so on—and they all serve chicken!

Because the three authors are experienced deans and have had numerous opportunities to make mistakes and learn from them, we decided this would be an excellent time for us to add our own choicest tidbits of "best advice" for beginners and those aspiring to become deans:

Dee: My best advice, especially for women aspiring to be leaders, is learn to lose. Even when you are right, you will lose a lot of fights—and some battles. It is important not to take your losses personally or to let them impede you from trying again. Too often we think not coming out on top is a reflection of our ability. It isn't.

Sandy: Take control of your calendar. Select two days a week, such as Tuesday and Thursday, and don't let anyone put something on your calendar—except, of course, the president or provost. You will find these days get filled anyway, but they provide you with some flexibility.

Take care of your staff as well as your faculty. They are the ones who will be there for you and provide assistance when you most need it.

Walt: Don't take conflict personally. Conflict comes with your position and is inherent in your role and woven into the fabric of higher education through bureaucratic rules, competing roles, differentiated rewards, and our hierarchical structure. Although you aren't responsible for some of these inherent conflicts woven into your institution, you are responsible for how you act and handle it.

It is important to note that throughout the interviews it became apparent that the preparation, development, and socialization of academic leaders appear to be left to chance. Although this may be a strategy in itself, institutions must realize the impact this can have on the dean's productivity and propensity toward longevity or departure from their institutions. It is our hope that this inquiry into the seasons of a dean's career helps illuminate the way to build and retain college leadership.

The Call for Developing Deans for All Seasons

To become an expert takes time. Studies of executives in the corporate world who attain international levels of performance point to the 10-year rule of preparation (Ericsson, Krampe, & Tesch-Romer, 1993); other studies estimate 10,000 hours of practice (Gladwell, 2008). Deans are no different, but they serve only six years on average, with many not even reaching the fall season of "keeping the fire alive." The lines of dean succession seem fairly clear, but the relatively high turnover rates suggest that we do not groom our leaders in ways that promote longevity, success, and effectiveness. For this reason alone, higher education can ill afford not to be attentive to preparing, advancing, and transitioning deans. Today, as never before, universities and colleges must answer the call to develop their leaders.

The studies conclude with the realization that leadership talent in universities is in scarce supply. Dean search committees often find their candidate pools resembling wading pools (Andersen, 2002). Those individuals who finally accept the position as dean have a terrible time balancing their personal and professional time and balancing their academic and administrative interests. Some of the imbalance stems from structural problems inherent in how universities are managed and organized. Other imbalances come from universities' inattention to the professional development of deans. These leaders need to be developed, supported, and balanced. It is a well-established fact that few deans receive preparation to conceptually understand and professionally balance the duties of their position. Yet the cost of leadership is too great not to invest in the most critical position of a university, the academic college chief executive officer.

Developing faculty into effective deans should be both a privilege and a responsibility of university administrators. Finding balance for these leaders should be a reciprocal relationship, because it requires both the institution's commitment and the faculty's receptivity to truly develop strong leadership. In our opinion, our study makes the case for the establishment of systematic leadership development programs for all levels of institutional administrators (for leadership development examples see Beineke & Sublett, 1999; Boyatzis, 1990; Conger, 1992; Conger & Benjamin, 1999; Green & McDade, 1994; Sessa & Taylor, 2000). The future of universities and colleges depends on answering the call with commitment and balance.

Conclusion

Throughout these pages we've summarized the views and experiences of formally interviewed deans as well as those who participated in semi-formal and informal conversations on their experiences as deans. Our own experiences as deans with a collective 50 years in the role across 10 deanships are embedded in the text as well. These interviews clearly show the extent to which a deanship can take over a life. The role of dean comes with a 7-day a week work commitment accompanied by evening events and multiple out-of-town trips. As one dean cited in chapter 2 emphatically said, "Being a dean is the best job I've ever had, but for you to work as hard as you will have to as a dean, you better love the job!" We all entered the position without formal training and only rarely with a mentor. We freely admit we made mistakes, but we did a lot right. Our driving force was a deep commitment to improving our colleges or departments of education, participating in the governance of our universities, and taking on political roles at the state and national level that we had never anticipated. We varied in our own and our families responses to our positions. At the end of the day, however, the deans who made it past the spring and summer seasons and into the fall agree that it is the best job we ever had.

References

Andersen, D. A. (2002). The deans of the future. In W. H. Gmelch (Ed.), *Deans balancing act: Education leaders and the challenges they face.* Washington, DC: AACTE Publications

Beineke, J. A., & Sublett, R. H. (1999). *Leadership lessons and competencies: Learning from the Kellogg National Fellowship Program.* Battle Creek, MI: Kellogg Foundation.

Bolman, L. G., & Deal, T. E. (2008). *Reframing organizations,* 4th ed. San Francisco: Jossey-Bass.

Boyatzis, R. (1990). *Beyond competence: The choice to be a leader.* Paper presented at the Academy of Management Meetings, San Francisco.

Collins, J. C., & Porras, J. I. (1994). *Built to last: Successful habits of visionary companies.* New York: Harper Business.

Conger, J. A. (1992). *Learning to lead: The art of transforming managers into leaders.* San Francisco: Jossey-Bass.

Conger, J. A., & Benjamin, B. (1999). *Building leaders: How successful companies develop the next generation.* San Francisco: Jossey-Bass.

Ericsson, K. A., Krampe, R. T., & Tesch-Romer, C. (1993). The role of deliberate practices in the acquisition of expert performance. *Psychological Review, 100*(3), 363–406.

Ericsson, K. A., & Smith, J. (1991). *Towards a general theory of expertise.* Cambridge: Cambridge University Press.

Gladwell, M. (2008). *Outliers: The story of success.* New York: Little, Brown and Company.

Gmelch, W. H., Reason, R. D., Schuh, J. H., & Shelley, M. C. (2002). *The call for academic leaders: The Academic Leadership Forum.* Ames: Iowa State University, Center for Academic Leadership.

Green, M. F., & McDade, S. A. (1994). *Investing in higher education: A handbook of leadership development.* Phoenix, AZ: Oryx Press.

Kouzes, J. M., & Posner, B. Z. (1987). *The leadership challenge: How to get extraordinary things done in organizations.* San Francisco: Jossey-Bass.

Schon, D. A. (1983). *The reflective practitioner: How professionals think in action.* New York: Basic Books.

Sessa, V. I., & Taylor, J. J. (2000). *Executive selection: Strategies for success.* San Francisco: Jossey-Bass.

Wolverton, M., & Gmelch, W. H. (2002). *College deans: Leading from within.* Westwood, CT: Oryx Press.

skill development, and leadership development, 8, 8*f,* 9–10
skill set, and applicant pools, 5–6
spouse. *See* family issues
spring deans
   on deanship, 24–28
   fall deans' advice for, 47–49
   winter deans' advice for, 78–81
springtime, 19–28
   dean loop and, 38–39, 38*f*
   term, 1
staff, winter deans on, 60–61, 80
students, summer deans on, 33
summer, 29–36
   dean loop and, 38*f,* 39
   term, 1

time management issues
   spring deans on, 24, 27
   summer deans on, 32
   winter deans on, 53–54, 56–57, 64–65,
      79–80
tinker tactics, 44–45

toehold tactics, 45–46
tradeoffs, 52–65
   definition of, 53
   internal-external, 58–62
   personal and professional, 53–56
   psychological, 62–65
   scholarship and leadership, 56–58
tyranny of competence, 38*f,* 44

Vaillant, George, 3
van Gennep, Arnold, 11–12
voice, finding, 77
Vygotsky, Lev, 44

winter, 51–68
   and advice to new deans, 78–81
   dean loop and, 38*f,* 39
   entering, 49
   term, 1

zigzag deans, 46–47
zone of proximal development, 44